Tricky Dick Nixon's Dirty Trickster
By CL Gammon

The cover image is in public domain.

For Rick Knox and Don Webb – America lost two great Patriots when Rick and Don passed on.

Acknowledgments

When I began researching this book, I contacted Donald Segretti. At first, he didn't want to have anything to do with this project. In an email to me he wrote, "As you may have gathered, I have gone on with my life and am reluctant to relive the events of those months."

Yet, he eventually agreed to answer (partially) some of my questions. It marked one of the very few times he has agreed to speak about his activities on the behalf of Nixon nearly a half century ago.

I cannot say that our communications were always cordial, but Segretti did provide me with some insights into his actions and his character. I am grateful to Segretti for agreeing to respond to some of my questions.

Mr. Gordon Weil also agreed to provide some insights into the 1972 election. Gordon served as Executive Assistant to Democratic presidential nominee George McGovern, and later, National Campaign Director for the McGovern campaign in 1972.

I am grateful to Gordon for being so generous with his time and for allowing me to impose upon him with a bevy of questions about the 1972 election.

Finally, I'd like to thank Kim Gammon for her work in editing this book.

Table of Contents

Introduction

Donald Henry Segretti did not look much like an agent provocateur. The diminutive Segretti stood about 5' 4" and weighed maybe 150 pounds. In addition, the seemingly meek, dark-haired, baby-faced lawyer appeared much younger than he actually was. Although, he was in his early thirties, Segretti could have passed for a high school student. When revealed as a dirty trickster, many who saw him for the first time could not believe that this meek "kid" could be involved in anything notorious – a panty raid maybe, but not political sabotage.

Yet, despite the first impressions, Segretti ran a large, illicit, and covert dirty tricks operation for the Nixon campaign in 1972.

Perhaps Segretti was born to be a dirty trickster. In Italian, Segretti means secretive, sneaking, and underhanded, and he was all those things; but whether he was born to it or not, Segretti was a natural at hardball politics and he was adept at political chicanery. This made him quite useful to Nixon. That is, until found out, then Segretti became just one more political liability for the beleaguered President.

However, Segretti does not hold the responsibility for his dirty tricks operation alone. One cannot look at the crimes committed by Segretti and others without considering the environment in which they worked – an environment created by President Richard Milhous Nixon.

Nixon always portrayed himself as a "law and order President." Yet, a blatant, callous, cynical, corrupt, and criminal disregard for the law marked his actions during his tenure. Nixon had a streak of paranoia running so deeply that it touched his very soul. He trusted almost no one and his lack of trust in others colored everything he did. He remained an isolated loner until the very end.

Despite opinion polls showing him in good shape for reelection in 1972, Nixon had a pathological fear of suffering an embarrassing political defeat that would render him a laughingstock. He was terrified that the continuing war in Vietnam, coupled with a weak economy, would doom him to be a one-term President – "another Hoover." Nixon was determined to defeat his opponents and win a second term – by any means necessary.

Nixon had a genuine disregard for the American democratic system. That coupled with his willingness to do practically anything to survive the 1972 election made Watergate and the other political crimes committed on his behalf almost inevitable. Beyond that, sabotaging the campaigns of his opponents was consistent with his self-image as a bare-knuckle street fighter – a "tough guy."

The fully staffed and generously funded dirty tricks organization, called the "campaign attack group" operating in Nixon's White House acted almost as a Cabinet Department would. Founded in 1969, Nixon's campaign attack group was the most extensive and effective dirty tricks apparatus ever established in American government.

Donald Segretti operated and, for a time, thrived in the environment created by Nixon. Had Nixon not encouraged, indeed demanded, a dirty trickster be hired, there would have been no place for a person of Segretti's toxic talents in the campaign.

This book deals with the actions of Donald Segretti and his network of dirty tricksters only. However, his was just one of a group of large, overlapping covert operations designed to undermine and defeat Nixon's political opponents.

The author invites the reader to learn as much about these interdependent dirty tricks operations functioning for Nixon's reelection as possible. If we would have our nation avoid other Watergate-type scandals and the damage such scandals cause our society, it behooves us to remember the excesses of the Nixon Administration.

1. What Are Dirty Tricks?

This author defines dirty tricks as efforts by one political campaign to damage one or more opposing campaigns, usually by clandestine means.

Usually, dirty tricks amount to the spreading of lies, rumors, and innuendo intended to damage a particular opponent. However, true information can fall in the realm of dirty tricks as well.

During its investigation, the Senate Watergate Committee called many Nixon aides to testify. Speechwriter and Special Assistant to President Nixon, Patrick "Pat" Buchanan, was one of the more enlightening witnesses. Buchanan was a member of the first White House dirty tricks team that Nixon ordered created on July 21, 1969. (The other members of the team were presidential assistants Lyn Nofziger and Clark Mollenhoff, the President's personal Secretary Rosemary Woods, and the Director of White House Communications, Herb Klein.)

Even though he produced a good deal of the material Segretti used in his dirty tricks operation, authorities never charged Buchanan with any crime in either the Watergate matter, or the dirty tricks campaign that preceded it. A darling of the conservatives, Buchanan has remained a major media and political figure for the past half century.

Evidently, Buchanan had given dirty tricks activities a lot of thought. He told the Senate

Committee that, in his opinion, there were "four gradations" of fringe campaign activities. Buchanan listed the gradations from worst to best as follows: (1) "Things that are certainly utterly outrageous"; (2) "Dirty tricks"; (3) "Political hardball"; and (4) "Pranks".

Buchanan did not define the four gradations in detail, but it is safe to say Segretti and his flunkies did things that touched all four of them. Segretti said of his activities, "they cover the whole gamut." Then, Segretti agreed with Senator Joseph Montoya (Democrat from New Mexico) that most of his activities were "dirty tricks" rather than "pranks." Segretti crossed the line into the realm of the "utterly outrageous" as well.

Dirty tricks have been around as along as politics has been around and politics has been around forever. The Roman city of Pompeii suffered destruction in 79 AD when the Mount Vesuvius erupted and covered the city in volcanic ash. 79 AD just happened to be an election year in Pompeii. Centuries later, as archeologists dug through the ashes and rubble of the poor, unfortunate city, they found several political slogans etched on its walls.

Some of the slogans found in the long dead city of Pompeii included:

"VOTE FOR VATIUS, ALL THE WHOREMONGERS VOTE FOR HIM."

"VOTE FOR VATIUS, ALL THE DRUNKS AND SLUG-A-BEDS VOTE FOR HIM."

VOTE FOR VATIUS, ALL THE WIFE-BEATERS ARE VOTING FOR HIM."

The United States has always been fertile ground for political skullduggery. The first contested presidential elections in the United States were no-holds-barred battles between John Adams and Thomas Jefferson. In 1800, loyal supporters of Jefferson (in those days, the candidates stood above the fray) claimed President Adams possessed a "hideous hermaphroditical character, which has neither the force and firmness of a man, nor the gentleness and sensibility of a woman."

Those speaking for President Adams responded that Vice President Jefferson was "a mean-spirited, low-lived fellow, the son of a half-breed Indian squaw, sired by a Virginia mulatto father." The campaign rhetoric only grew worse after that.

In the 1820s, John Quincy Adams and Andrew Jackson were involved in mudslinging so vile that even today this author despairs to repeat some of it in "polite company."

The dirty tricks and mudslinging has not abated throughout the years. While there are hundreds of examples, a few should illustrate that the practice has remained alive and well in American, and continues even today.

In 1964, officials in the Johnson Administration pushing for the reelection of the President formed what they called the "Five O'clock Club." Club members met in the White House every afternoon and formulated dirty tricks for use against Republican presidential nominee, Senator Barry Goldwater of Arizona. Many dirty tricks formulated by the Five O'clock Club were very effective.

Richard "Dick" Tuck was a poisoned thorn in Richard Nixon's side. Tuck was a political operative of the Democratic Party who unleashed dirty tricks and pranks against several Republicans, but Nixon was his favorite target. Tuck drew a great deal of attention, and praise (from the Democrats) by pranking Nixon on several occasions.

Pat Buchanan described a few of the high-profile "pranks" Tuck played on Nixon. Buchanan said, "I recall just three, briefly three of his favorites.

"One of them was in 1962 when Mr. Nixon began to deliver a major address from the back of a railroad train he put on an engineer's cap and signaled the engineer to drive off leaving Mr. Nixon standing there.

"Another of his favorites was during a major political speech just as the speaker reaches the denouement he drops the fire escape.

"The third was, we were at the Hilton Hotel down there in Miami Beach, and out in front demonstrating – I thought it was welfare mothers or we were told it was welfare mothers at the time – they were all black, they were all pregnant, and they were all carrying placards that said, 'NIXON'S THE ONE.'"

One would have thought that after the exposure the Watergate scandal generated, and the eventual resignation of President Nixon, candidates would have forbidden dirty tricks operations in their campaigns, but this has not proven to be the case. In 1988, agents working on the behalf of Democratic presidential candidate, Massachusetts Governor, Michael S. Dukakis, exposed the truth that Delaware Senator, Joseph Biden, as a plagiarist.

The Governor's agents didn't stop with attempting to wreck the Biden campaign by exposing him, however. They released false information that another leading candidate for the 1988 Democratic nomination, Missouri Representative Richard Gephardt, was guilty of outing Biden. The false story threw the Gephardt campaign off stride. Neither Biden nor Gephardt recovered from the dirty tricks and Dukakis won the Democratic nomination.

As with the case related above, sometimes dirty tricksters release true information about candidates timed to cause the greatest amount of damage possible. For instance, the revelation just before the November election in 2000 that George W. Bush had gotten a DUI many years earlier was true, but a dirty trick nonetheless.

Of course, some dirty tricks backfire. In 2004, CBS News ran a story that featured fraudulent memorandums designed to throw aspersions on President George W. Bush's military record. The dirty trick unraveled and CBS fired long-time reporter, Dan Rather, because of his involvement in the incident. The dirty trick, called "memo-gate" actually helped the Bush reelection bid.

The dirty tricks continue today. In fact, presently, American presidential politics is often more dirty trick than truth.

2. Segretti's Early Life

Donald Henry Segretti was born into a hardworking, middleclass family in San Marino, California on September 17, 1941. He had a typical childhood.

Segretti was very bright and he proved to be a good student. He graduated from the University of Southern California in 1963 with a degree in finance, and he graduated from the law school at the University of California, at Berkeley in 1966. He was a member of the Phi Sigma Kappa fraternity.

Segretti was active in college and he was a member of a collegiate organization called the "Trojans for Representative Government." During his association with this group, he engaged in some, mostly sophomoric, pranks during campus elections. According to the best information available, "Ballot boxes were stuffed, spies were planted in the opposition camp, and bogus campaign literature abounded."

After law school, Segretti traveled across the country to take a job as an attorney in the Office of the Comptroller of Currency in Washington, D.C. He liked working so close to America's power center.

Segretti's civilian career went on hold in May 1967, when he submitted to the military draft and induction into the United States Army. He applied for, and received a commission in the Judge Advocate Corps and served as a military prosecutor.

Segretti remained in the Army for four years and four months, including one year in Vietnam serving with American Division headquarters in Chulai and U.S. Army Vietnam headquarters at Longbinh. He received an Honorable Discharge in September 1971. Some of the awards the military bestowed on Segretti were a Bronze Star, the Army Commendation Medal, and the Air Medal.

While in the Army, Segretti proved himself a solid attorney while acting as a military prosecutor.

He went almost straight from soldier to political trickster.

3. Segretti Joins the Team

President Richard Nixon often ranted to his Appointments Secretary, Dwight Chapin, about politics. Nixon confided to Chapin that the Republicans needed an individual to do "Dick Tuck-type things" in 1972. Whether Nixon was serious about finding a Republican Dick Tuck or not, Chapin took the President's remarks as a direct order and began the process of honoring it.

Chapin got together with aide to White House Chief of Staff, H. R. Haldeman, Gordon Strachan and the two discussed the possibility of a "dirty tricks" field operation in 1972. They thought it would be ideal to develop a dirty tricks apparatus outside the White House and apart from the operation Special Council to the President, Charles "Chuck" Colson already had up and running.

Chapin and Strachan pegged their old college chum from the University of Southern California named Donald Segretti to lead the dirty tricks operation. They knew Segretti was a good prankster and that he had engaged in political pranks while attending college.

They envisioned Segretti disrupting the various Democratic presidential campaigns by pulling pranks on them. There is no evidence that Chapin or Strachan ordered Segretti to engage in any illegal activities, but they should have known that the area is gray and the line is thin, between political pranks and criminal acts.

Chapin contacted his old friend in April 1971 about a possible job when Segretti got out of the Army. Segretti was interested in the job, even though he did not know exactly what he might be doing. In fact, Segretti had called Strachan sometime before Chapin contacted him about possible employment. Segretti was keen on taking the job because, as he put it:

"I was happy to accept employment from people who held prominent positions in and out of the government. I was in agreement with President's announced policies of ending the Vietnam War and the draft. Thus, it was on principle that I favored his reelection. It was something to do."

Segretti was also interested because (1) he thought the job Chapin offered might bring him some excitement to his drab postwar life, and (2) he believed Nixon would reward him with a good job in the White House after the election.

In June 1971, Segretti flew to Washington D.C. and met with Chapin and Strachan on two separate occasions. The first meeting took place at a dinner party at Chapin's house, and the second took place the next day at lunch. During these meetings, Chapin and Strachan briefed Segretti on the nature of the tasks they intended for him to perform. They explained that they wanted him to pull off political pranks designed to aid in President Nixon's reelection. While Chapin and Strachan did not formally offer the job to Segretti at that time, they thought they had their fish on the hook.

As the meeting ended, Strachan handed Segretti $400 in cash to cover his travel expenses, then he and Chapin asked Segretti not to discuss the matter with anyone. However, Segretti was excited and soon after the meeting, he contacted several old friends and told them he had the opportunity to work in the Nixon campaign. This was the first indication that Segretti might be a weak link in the White House espionage and sabotage operations.

Chapin and Strachan still needed approval to launch their dirty tricks operation against the Democrats. The two men presented their operational plan to the President's Chief of Staff H. R. Haldeman and he approved of it on the spot. Haldeman said later, "I agreed that if this man wanted to take on this activity, Herb Kalmbach [the President's personal attorney] should arrange for his compensation and expenses from the 1968 campaign fund surplus." Haldeman continued, "It was my clear understanding that Segretti would act independently and on his own initiative within broad guidelines" outlined by his handlers. In addition, Haldeman emphasized that, "It was my clear understanding that he was to engage in no illegal acts." Strachan assured Haldeman that Segretti understood that everything he did must be legal.

In early summer of 1971 Chapin, Strachan, Pat Buchanan, staff assistant Ken Khachigian, and head of White House advance operations Ron Walker, engaged in a meeting on the structure of Segretti's dirty tricks operation. Buchanan stressed that "it should be a small operation and . . . it ought to be under the Committee to Reelect the President." The others agreed.

The Committee to Reelect the President was the organization tasked with carrying on Nixon's 1972 campaign. The Committee had chapters in virtually every state and city in the United States.

It is unclear how many of those that took part in this meeting knew of the "intelligence gathering" operation G. Gordon Liddy and E. Howard Hunt already had up and running. What is certain is that there was no discussion of linking the two enterprises together at that time. The linkage happened later.

Once the project received Haldeman's enthusiastic blessing, Strachan told Segretti to go to Newport Beach, California, contact Herbert "Herb" Kalmbach, and finalize his employment. Segretti and Kalmbach met in late August 1971.

Kalmbach offered Segretti an annual salary of $16,000 (almost $100,000 in today's currency), which was not a bad sum for the time. In addition, Kalmbach promised to reimburse Segretti for all his expenses. Segretti was unemployed at the time and he was more than happy to accept the deal Kalmbach offered him. In fact, he would have accepted considerably less than $16,000 annually.

(Note: Throughout this book, the author provides dollar amounts. They may seem paltry and insignificant by today's standards,

but one must remember that one dollar in 1972 was worth more than six of today's dollars.)

Following his meeting with Kalmbach, Segretti lunched with Chapin near President Nixon's "Western White House" in San Clemente, California. During this leisurely meeting, Chapin detailed exactly what he wanted Segretti to do. Chapin described Segretti's mission as a part of "a common campaign strategy" employed by both parties. Then he passed a list of cities and states to Segretti with instructions to concentrate on them during the presidential primaries. The most important states on the list were New Hampshire, Florida, Illinois, Wisconsin, Pennsylvania, Ohio, Indiana, California, New Jersey, New York, and Texas.

Chapin placed a great deal of emphasis on secrecy. Segretti said Chapin told him "not to use the names of any persons at the White House or the name of any person associated with the Republican Party when making my contacts." Segretti continued that he was "not to use my real name so that I would never prove an embarrassment to the President or his campaign supporters." Segretti told Chapin he understood his orders.

Chapin laid a brief game plan for Segretti to follow:

(1) Go after Muskie: Chapin instructed Segretti to concentrate his activities on damaging United States Senator from Maine, Edmund G. Muskie. Muskie, the 1968

Democratic Party nominee for Vice President was the frontrunner for the 1972 Democratic presidential nomination. Chapin explained that if he could seriously weaken Muskie, Segretti would improve President Nixon's chances of winning reelection dramatically.

There is no doubt that of the announced candidates, President Nixon feared Muskie the most. As one political commentator pointed out, Muskie had "ample financial backing, name recognition, experience, image, endorsements, and top standing in the polls." The perception was that Muskie would roll to the Democratic nomination. Chapin ordered Segretti to help change that perception and Segretti felt he was up to the task.

(2) Create Bitterness: Chapin instructed Segretti to create bitterness and mistrust among the various Democratic candidates. Chapin explained that by splitting the Democratic candidates Segretti could help prevent the Democratic Party from uniting behind the eventual nominee.

(3) Use the Media: Chapin encouraged Segretti to attempt to utilize television, radio, newspapers, and other forms of media – national and local – to his advantage. Chapin suggested that Segretti do things such as have demonstrators with Humphrey signs show up at Muskie events. In addition, Chapin said that Segretti should issue phony press releases whenever he could.

Following the California meeting with Chapin, Segretti got right to work. He began contacting old friends in California, old Army comrades, and others about doing "political work" with him in 1972. However, he did not provide his prospective contacts much information, at least not at first. He wanted them to be with him before he revealed the true nature of what they would be doing. Of course, more than a few of those Segretti contacted would not commit to anything without knowing their prospective tasks and he had to go into some detail to get his prospective dirty tricksters aboard his dastardly train.

Below is an example of the explanation Segretti gave to a recruit:

"For instance, we'll go to a Kennedy rally and find an ardent Kennedy worker. Then you say that you're a Kennedy man too but you're working behind the scenes; you get them to help you. You send them to work for Muskie, stuffing envelopes or whatever, and you get them to pass you the information. They'll think that they are helping Kennedy against Muskie. But actually you're using the information for something else."

Segretti promised recruits good jobs within the administration after the election. He told those he wanted to draw into his web, "Nixon knows that something is being done. It is a typical deal. 'Don't tell me anything and I won't talk.'"

Segretti later said, ". . . I had no knowledge whether . . . the President knew anything that I did."

Chapin didn't mind his old friend getting to work early, but Chapin wanted Segretti better armed for the task ahead of him.

After his discharge on September 13, 1971, Segretti received a call from Chapin. During the course of this call, Chapin informed Segretti that Strachan was no longer involved in the operation. Chapin also informed Segretti that in the future they would use aliases when leaving messages for each other. Segretti would be "Don Morris and Chapin would be "Bob Duane." However, Chapin actually used the code name "Chapman" most of the time and Segretti sometimes used the names "Don Durham" and "Don Simmons."

Chaplin requested Segretti catch a flight to Washington, D.C. and meet with him on September 23, 1971. Segretti complied and the two met in the dining room of the Hays-Adams Hotel in downtown Washington. During their meal, Chapin instructed Segretti to rent a post office box from which he could receive mail related to the operation. Chapin also told Segretti to get an answering service so that Chapin could reach him at all times.

As the dinner was ending, Chapin slipped Segretti an envelope containing a list of Nixon advance men from 1968. Chapin advised Segretti to use the list and begin quickly making contacts in the appropriate primary states. Once again, Chapin stressed as strongly as he could that Segretti never say or do anything that could link the operation to Chapin, to the White House, to the Republican Party, or to the Committee to Reelect the President.

Chapin also gave Segretti the name of Ward Turnquist. Turnquist was an old high school of Chapin's and Chapin thought Turnquist would make a good contact for Segretti in southern California.

Chapin desired for Segretti to understand how a political advance team worked. Chapin envisioned Segretti as running a "black advance team." An advance team makes sure that a political event goes smoothly; a black advance team makes sure a political event goes roughly.

Chapin directed Segretti to fly to Portland, Oregon the following day (September 24, 1971) ahead of the President's visit there. Chapin ordered Segretti to observe a political advance operation up close. Segretti agreed and he flew to Portland and took a room at the Benson Hotel. While in Portland, Segretti became familiar with how an advance team worked and how an advance team dealt with problems such as demonstrators. He also developed some ideas on how to disrupt a political event.

Additionally, while in Portland, Segretti called the local District Attorney and asked him for the name of "anyone that might want to get involved in political activity." The District Attorney supplied Segretti with a name, but he was not interested in joining the dirty tricks team.

On Sunday morning, September 26, Chapin visited Segretti at the Benson Hotel. The two men sat in Segretti's room and continued their discussion on Segretti's assignment. Before Chapin left, he passed on a copy of the *Advanceman's Manual* to Segretti.

After the meeting with Chapin, Segretti checked out of the Benson Hotel and caught a flight to Los Angeles for a meeting with Herb Kalmbach. During that meeting (on September 29), Kalmbach handed Segretti an envelope containing two checks. One check was a $5,000 advance on Segretti's expenses. The second check, this one for $667, covered Segretti's first two weeks salary.

Following Nixon's visit to Portland, Chapin mailed a memo to Segretti. The memo stated:

"From now on, we want to have at least one Muskie sign in amongst the demonstrators who are demonstrating against the President. It should be "Muskie for President" and should be held in a location so it is clearly visible.

"At Muskie events or events by other Democratic hopefuls, there should be a sign or two which goads them. For example, at a Muskie rally, there should be a large 'Why Not a Black Vice President' or perhaps 'We prefer Humphrey' or something else that would goad him along.

"At Humphrey rallies there should be Muskie signs, and so on. These signs should be well placed in relationship to the press area so that a picture is easy to get."

4. Segretti Causes Problems

Ready for action, and aching to make history, Donald Segretti embarked upon his mission and entered into the dark world of illicit hardball political combat.

Donald Segretti was enthusiastic about his mission – too much so at times. His efforts soon caused problems for those in the service of which he toiled.

As Segretti felt his way through, he maintained steady contact with Chapin. Between the beginning of November 1971 and the end of January of 1972, Segretti telephoned Chapin at least thirty-three times. On several occasions, Chapin told Segretti he wanted him to act independently and without supervision, but the amount of contact between the two indicates that Chapin had almost total control of the Segretti operation – at least in its early stages.

Chapin ordered Segretti to perform several individual tasks. For instance, Chapin alerted Segretti that Senator Muskie would be in Los Angeles in November 1971. Chapin instructed Segretti to round up some individuals, give them anti-Muskie signs, and have them heckle the Senator. A few days after the Los Angeles event, Chapin ordered Segretti to position demonstrators outside a San Francisco hotel where Muskie and Senator Humphrey had a scheduled appearance at a Democratic Party dinner.

The first bit of trouble for Segretti came in connection with an event Muskie attended at Nixon's alma mater, Whittier College. In an effort to disrupt the event, Segretti prepared a list of "hard questions" for those in the crowd to ask Senator Muskie. Segretti passed the questions out among the audience and at least one audience member asked one of the questions Segretti had planted about abortion.

Despite Segretti's efforts, Muskie handled the situation at Whittier well. In fact, Segretti's operation may have actually helped Muskie. Shortly after the event, an unhappy Chapin mailed Segretti a copy of a report consisting of a rundown of recent media stories called "The White House News Summary." The report quoted Frank Reynolds of ABC News as saying that Muskie "had come prepared for conservative questions but the Chicanos gave him no chance and Big Ed proved that he can keep his cool."

Chapin penciled a notation in the margin of the summary, "Note we really missed the boat on this – obviously the press now wants to prove EM can keep his temper – let's prove he can't."

Another problem came out of the Muskie event in California. A group of individuals threw eggs at Muskie and his staff. The egg-throwing incident represented direct violence against a candidate and the White House did not want it repeated. Shortly thereafter, Strachan called Segretti and asked him directly if he orchestrated the egg-throwing incident. Even though Segretti denied any responsibility for the egg throwing, it lowered his standing among those White House staffers that were aware of his activities.

Segretti next encountered a problem in the first primary state, New Hampshire. In early November 1971, Chapin instructed Segretti to go to New Hampshire and to establish a dirty tricks operation there. In order to move the process along, Chapin gave Segretti the name of the New Hampshire State Chair of the Committee to Reelect the President, Allen Walker. Segretti and Walker hit it off immediately. Segretti found Walker to be "a very personable and likable gentleman."

Segretti believed that Walker was interested in helping in New Hampshire and Segretti provided Walker with some of the details of the dirty tricks he had planned for the Granite State. Segretti felt so at ease with Walker, that he revealed his real name.

Evidently, Walker was not as impressed with Segretti as Segretti was with Walker. Walker called around Washington in an attempt to find out who this man Segretti was and his true motives. Walker's inquiries made their way to the White House and to Chapin.

Shortly after Walker began inquiring about Segretti, the trickster received a phone call from an incensed Chapin. Chapin ordered Segretti to get out of New Hampshire immediately and to catch the next available flight to Washington D.C. Segretti followed his orders and flew to Washington. Upon arriving, he took a hotel room near the airport. Soon thereafter, a still angry Chapin visited him.

Chapin chewed out Segretti and told him that he could have compromised the entire dirty tricks operation by confiding his real name to Walker. Chapin ordered Segretti to stay out of New Hampshire from then on and he cautioned Segretti never to use his true name again with anyone involved with the reelection campaign.

Despite his anger and concern, Chapin never considered firing Segretti and shutting the dirty tricks campaign down. Neither did Chapin specifically restrict Segretti from doing things in New Hampshire from a distance.

When Dwight Chapin and Gordon Strachan first got together and discussed the Segretti dirty tricks operation, they agreed that it should remain divorced from the White House. They understood that the closer the operation was to the President, the more dangerous it was for him. Yet, after Strachan left the plot, by managing Segretti so closely, Chapin tied the operation to himself and to the White House.

Chapin was not aware of the details of all of Segretti's dirty tricks, but he knew a great deal about most of them. Segretti mailed copies of most of the literature, campaign materials (bumper stickers, signs, cards, etc.), and fake letters to Chapin's residence in Washington. Additionally, Segretti informed Chapin of his most obnoxious dirty tricks. These included the Muskie busing poster, the letter smearing US Senator from Washington, Henry Jackson and former Vice President Hubert Humphrey sent under the Muskie letterhead, and the fake Humphrey press release accusing US

Representative from New York, Shirley Chisholm of spending time in an insane asylum. (The author details these and many other dirty tricks Donald Segretti and his team perpetrated in later chapters.)

Along with the other items, Segretti mailed newspaper clippings that the dirty tricks field operation engendered. Segretti was proud of his pranks and sent hand-written notes weekly to Chapin outlining his antics.

While Segretti sometimes exasperated him, Chapin was usually positive and encouraging when he communicated to his old friend. At no time did Chapin and Segretti ever discuss the legality of any of the dirty tricks performed. Chapin said that since Segretti was an attorney, he believed the dirty trickster would never cross the line into criminality.

Despite the fact that Chapin recruited Segretti and was his direct contact, the President's Appointment Secretary simply could not keep Segretti under proper control. The complaints continued.

In the three-month period between December 1971 and February 1972, Segretti did almost as much to disrupt the Republican effort in the field as to damage the Democratic effort. There was a bevy of complaints from individuals to Republican organizations such as the Young Republicans, the College Republicans, and the Young Voters for the President. There groups transmitted their complaints to Bart Porter, Tom Bell, and Ken Rietz of the Committee to Reelect the

President. Porter, Bell, and Rietz passed the complaints on to a senior member of the Committee to Reelect the President, Jeb Magruder. The complaints related that there was an operative in the field causing serious problems for the reelection campaign.

One of the more serious complaints against Segretti originated with Tom Gratz of Madison, Wisconsin. Gratz transmitted his concerns to the President-elect of the College Republicans, Carl Rove. Rove alerted the Committee to Reelect the President to the problem. Eventually, private investigator Anthony Ulasewicz received the assignment from John Ehrlichman to deal with Gratz's complaint. Ulasewicz flew to Wisconsin to discover the identity of this mysterious operative and to discern the exact scope of his mission.

Ulasewicz could not locate Segretti, but while he was in Wisconsin searching for the elusive troublemaker, Ulasewicz received a telephone call from another private investigator working for Ehrlichman, Jack Caulfield. Caulfield informed Ulasewicz that Segretti was an employee of the Committee to Reelect the President. At that, Ulasewicz ended his search and returned to Washington.

5. Enter Liddy and Hunt

The large number of complaints he received about Segretti concerned Jeb Magruder. In January 1972, Magruder wrote a long memorandum to chair of the Nixon reelection campaign, John Mitchell. Mitchell, who also served as Attorney General of the United States, had intimate knowledge of the dirty tricks operation headed by G. Gordon Liddy and E. Howard Hunt then underway on behalf of the President.

Magruder titled the memo, "Matter of Potential Embarrassment." He described the problems Segretti was causing the Nixon campaign. Magruder contended that Chapin was not up to the task of supervising Segretti and the memorandum urged Mitchell to place Segretti under the direction of G. Gordon Liddy.

Liddy's title was General Council to the Committee to Reelect the President. However, his real job was leading intelligence gathering operations for the 1972 Nixon campaign. In connection with these operations, he was involved in various intelligence-sabotage operations commonly referred to as "offensive security" by the White House. His offensive security operations included criminal acts, including break-ins, bugging offices, and stealing documents.

Liddy was an old hand at illegal operations. Previously, he had been a member of the "White House Plumbers." This group had the task of plugging leaks, political and otherwise, coming out of the White House. While with the Plumbers, Liddy was involved in at least one high-profile burglary and he planned others, but his supervisors at the White House vetoed his requests for other burglaries.

The "Matter of Potential Embarrassment" memorandum made its way to the desk of White House Chief of Staff, H. R. Haldeman. Haldeman agreed with Magruder that G. Gordon Liddy could control Segretti better than could Chapin. Haldeman ordered Gordon Strachan to get in touch with Segretti and tell him to expect a call from Liddy. In addition, Haldeman told Strachan to inform Segretti that Liddy would give him instructions in the future.

Strachan had divorced himself from the Segretti operation months earlier and he did not want to become involved again. He passed Haldeman's instructions on to Dwight Chapin. The only other involvement Strachan had with the Segretti affair was that he followed Haldeman's orders after the Watergate break-in and shredded the "Matter of Potential Embarrassment" memorandum.

Also, in January 1972 (either in a phone call, or during their meeting in Washington on January 20), Chapin informed Segretti that the Nixon people in Washington were bothered by the problems Segretti had caused the Committee to Reelect the President in New Hampshire and Wisconsin. Chapin further told Segretti to prepare himself for a visit from "someone" representing the Nixon campaign.

This person, according to Chapin, would be checking on Segretti's operation. Chapin did not provide Segretti with the name of Segretti's visitor.

It is interesting to note that as of the latter days of January of 1972, Segretti had caused a great many headaches for the Committee to Reelect the President, apparently no one in the Nixon campaign gave any thought to firing him and shutting down his operation. It is obvious that those leading Nixon's various dirty tricks operations still viewed Segretti as a valuable asset – at least potentially.

In addition to the other complaints about Segretti, in January 1972, G. Gordon Liddy informed his working mate, CIA Agent, E. Howard Hunt, that he had information about an unknown Democrat. According to Liddy, this Democrat was attempting to worm his way in Republican headquarters in some primary states.

Intent upon identifying the infiltrator before he could cause any real damage, Liddy issued a communiqué to all state chapters of the Committee to Reelect the President. The dispatch included a physical description of the suspected infiltrator and a rundown of what the unidentified person had done so far. Liddy stressed that it was imperative for the state committees to remain vigilant, to locate the infiltrator, and to put an end to his "counter productive" activities.

Less than a week after Liddy issued the dispatch regarding the suspected infiltrator, he telephoned Hunt. Liddy said he had irritated some of the folk at the Committee to Reelect the President because the alleged infiltrator worked for them. Though Liddy did not identify anyone by name, Segretti was the person misidentified as an infiltrator.

A short time later, Liddy contacted Hunt, regarding Segretti yet again. Liddy relayed that one of those for whom Segretti worked had asked him to evaluate Segretti's work up to that point and then to pass that evaluation back to Segretti's White House bosses. Liddy continued that Segretti's handlers wanted his activities monitored and the young man provided with assistance. However, Liddy and Hunt were not to compromise their primary task of gathering intelligence on the Democratic candidates for President and the Democratic Party hierarchy.

Liddy assumed correctly, as it turned out, that Segretti's bosses wanted the prankster put under the umbrella of Liddy-Hunt dirty tricks operation. In addition, the White House wanted Libby and Hunt to assume at least partial responsibility for Segretti's activities.

A few days after Segretti's aforementioned conversation with Chapin, Segretti, who was in California, took a telephone call from a man calling himself Ed Warren. This man turned out to be E. Howard Hunt. Hunt identified himself as an official of the Committee to Reelect the President and he asked Segretti to meet with him as soon as possible. Segretti agreed to the meeting.

On February 11, 1972, Segretti caught a commercial flight and endured the long air trip from California to Miami. Then he took a taxi to an inexpensive motel nearby, and booked a single room. Then he called the number Hunt had given him and provided his room number to the man that answered.

On February 12, two men came up to Segretti's motel room and one of them banged one the door loudly. Segretti opened the door and allowed two men into the room. Hunt, looking dapper, clinching a pipe between his teeth, and still calling himself Ed Warren, entered first. Behind Hunt was a menacing man of forty-something who had piercing eyes, thinning black hair, and a bushy mustache. This man, identified himself as George Leonard, but was in truth, G. Gordon Liddy.

The ever-paranoid Hunt released a little puff of tobacco smoke from the corner of his mouth, and made a quick visual scan of the room. Then, he turned on the small television in the corner of and cranked up the volume as loud as it would go. This was Hunt's attempt to prevent anyone from listening in or recording the conversation. Hunt feared that either the room was bugged or that Segretti had a tape recorder hidden out of sight. Hunt should not have worried about the pale and diminutive Segretti.

The "tough guy" images Liddy and Hunt projected intimidated Segretti. He slowly and timidly explained that his operation consisted primarily of: (1) having protesters appear at rallies of Democratic candidates. These demonstrators carried signs supporting other Democratic candidates and (2) distributing phony pamphlets designed to embarrass various Democratic candidates and causing animosity between them.

Unimpressed with Segretti's "rat fucking" operation, Liddy and Hunt ordered Segretti to use fake identification with all his operatives, but they never provided him with any. Hunt did provide Segretti with the name of a Miami area printer named Joe Arriola. Hunt ordered Segretti to use Arriola for everything he had printed.

As the meeting ended, Liddy pulled Segretti aside and ordered the young man to follow all instructions to the letter. Liddy then made a direct threat. Liddy said Hunt would break Segretti's kneecaps if he did not comply with his instructions in absolute detail. Segretti took the warning seriously. From then on, Segretti belonged to Liddy and Hunt as well as Chapin.

The meeting with Liddy and Hunt only lasted 10 to 15 minutes, but it had an impact on Segretti. After that, Segretti so feared Hunt that he always followed "suggestions" Hunt gave him as if they were the law of the land.

While Hunt gave Segretti direction occasionally, Segretti continued to provide Chapin status reports and receive orders from him as well. Later, Segretti said he was not certain exactly who his bosses were. However, he evidently pleased Liddy and Hunt because they never broke his kneecaps. In addition, Segretti and Chapin remained in contact until the White House pulled the plug on the Segretti operation.

6. Segretti's Dirty Tricks

Donald Segretti's black advance team of pranksters and dirty trick artists were active throughout the United States. The scope of the Segretti operation was much more widespread than is generally imagined. According to documented travel records, Segretti flew to at least fifteen cities, some of them multiple times: Some of the cities Segretti visited in association with his dirty tricks operation included Albuquerque, Chicago, Houston, Knoxville, Los Angeles, Manchester, New Hampshire; Miami, Milwaukee, New York City, Portland, Oregon, Salt Lake City, San Francisco, Tampa, Tucson, and Washington, D.C.

While this book contains a large catalog of the dirty tricks Segretti committed and oversaw, it is not by any means a complete list. No one will ever discover some of the dirty tricks Segretti and his team perpetrated before the fallout from the failed Watergate break-in ended his activities.

Donald Segretti's operation was sloppy and at times haphazard, but despite how it appeared, especially to some members of the Committee to Reelect the President, Segretti was following a general plan of action Chapin had outlined for him. This plan, employing relatively few techniques, proved very effective when Segretti followed it correctly.

Segretti's tactical objectives were few, but rather wide in nature. In addition, they grew as time went along. One must understand that not all these objectives were set in stone, but evolved as time went along. Segretti devised some of them after a few beers or a couple glasses of wine.

Below is a short list of Segretti's tactical objectives as Chapin explained them to him:

(A) Infiltrate campaigns: Segretti received orders to infiltrate the campaigns of the candidates for the Democratic presidential nomination, to disrupt them, to gather intelligence and to foster division among the candidates.

(B) Spy on Nixon's Opponents: Segretti attempted to monitor the movements of the Democratic candidates. This included hiring private detectives to follow selected candidates from place to place.

(C) Disrupt Campaigns: Segretti attempted to disrupt the campaigns of all the major Democratic hopefuls – especially the Muskie campaign. If Segretti could cause confusion among the Democrats through his disruptive efforts, it would make Nixon's path to reelection much easier, or so Segretti and his masters thought.

(D) False Advertising: Segretti and his agents placed false or misleading advertisements on radio, and in newspapers. The intent of these ads was to create confusion among voters and to keep the various Democratic campaigns off balance and at odds with each other.

(E) Protesters: Segretti attempted to have protestors carrying easily identifiable signs to show up at rallies of the various Democratic candidates and take advantage of media coverage to cause disharmony among the Democratic candidates.

(F) Disrupt the Democratic national convention: Segretti intended to do a large number of things to disrupt the Democratic national convention, but he had to scuttle most of them due to the foiled Watergate burglary.

(G) Other Pranks and Dirty Tricks: Segretti also employed what at first blush one might consider sophomoric or even childish pranks to disrupt the various Democratic campaigns. While one might think the pranks funny if featured on a television sitcom, they were effective in reducing the efficiency of several of the Democratic campaigns.

In some states, Segretti's operation ran well. The chapters below provide a partial list of operations the Segretti team ran in various states. The listing of the states is by order of the primaries chronologically and the dirty tricks by type.

7. New Hampshire

Edmund Muskie of Maine was the media-anointed frontrunner for the nomination in 1972. From the time he entered the race, the Senator targeted New Hampshire as the state that would hand him an overwhelming victory and eliminate all his Democratic rivals. Then, Muskie planned to use the remainder of the primary season bringing the Democratic Party together and honing his attacks on President Nixon. His vision was to enter the fall campaign with a unified party behind him, with overwhelming momentum, and with an overflowing war chest at his disposal. However, Muskie's express train to the White House soon ran off the rails and Nixon's dirty tricks operatives had a lot to do with it.

Perhaps the most effective act of political sabotage from 1972 was the infamous "Canuck Letter." The most powerful newspaper in New Hampshire, the pro-Republican and deeply conservative *Manchester Union Leader* published the Canuck Letter on February 24, 1972, less than two weeks before the critical New Hampshire primary. The Canuck Letter alleged that Senator Edmund Muskie condoned an ethic slur made against Americans of French-Canadian extraction. The letter was one of the sparks that set off Muskie's famous "Crying Incident."

In addition to the Canuck Letter, the *Manchester Union Leader* reprinted an item that had appeared in *Time Magazine* on December 27, 1971. The story stated that while

Muskie's wife Jane was on a chartered bus, she shouted to reporters and aides, "Let's tell dirty jokes." The story, first reported by Jane Stroud of *Women's Wear Daily*, also contended that Jane Muskie used profane language, and drank heavily.

On February 26, 1972, Muskie gave an impassioned speech in front of the offices of the *Manchester Union Leader*. Shaking with emotion, Muskie made personal attacks against the paper's publisher, William Loeb. Among other things, Muskie called Loeb "gutless" and a "coward."

During his rant, Muskie appeared to break into tears. Muskie had a reputation as one who lacked the temperament to be President and his loss of control caused severe damage to his campaign. In addition, Muskie's childish behavior boosted the campaign of South Dakota Senator George McGovern.

The Muskie camp knew that the crying incident had damaged him. However, they believed his lead in New Hampshire was so large, and that the field against him was so weak, that he would still garner well over half the vote and would become the presumptive Democratic nominee. They also believed that by November the Crying Incident would be old news. Muskie's team was wrong.

Muskie did "win" the New Hampshire primary, but he fell far short of expectations. Muskie bested McGovern 41,235 (46.4%) to 33,007 (37.1%). The unexpected result sent shockwaves through Muskie's campaign and stunned his supporters. The surprise was such that the Muskie campaign could not fathom how to spin the result as anything but a debacle. The Muskie reaction to the result only made the situation worse.

America's media jumped on Muskie's failure and many pundits wondered openly if the Maine Senator could overcome the New Hampshire disaster. Donald Segretti's job was to make sure Muskie did not.

8. Was Segretti Responsible?

Before going forward, it is necessary to ask the question, "Was Segretti responsible for the Canuck Letter?"

The truth is that there is no "smoking gun" evidence proving that Donald Segretti or any of his henchmen produced the Canuck Letter. However, a good amount of circumstantial evidence indicating that Segretti may have been involved with the Canuck Letter does exist.

The Canuck letter carried the signature of Paul Morrison of Deerfield Beach, Florida and it carried a Florida postmark. No one ever located Morrison and it is obvious that no such person ever existed. This is proof positive that the Canuck Letter was a fake – a dirty trick. Since Segretti was very active in Florida at that time, and his handlers forbid him from returning to New Hampshire in person, it makes sense that he (or one of his henchmen) would have mailed the letter from the Sunshine State.

Another fact that points to Segretti is the letter itself. Misspellings and grammatical errors filled the letter. This was typical for a Segretti produced document. Many of the materials he transmitted feigned illiteracy.

Still another fact is that Muskie's meltdown was exactly what Chapin ordered Segretti to make happen. Dwight Chapin had written to Segretti, "Obviously the press now wants to prove EM [Edmund Muskie] can keep his temper – let's prove he can't." The crying incident proved positively that Muskie could not "keep his temper."

Further evidence that the Canuck letter was a dirty trick also exists. After Muskie had shot himself in the foot with his tantrum, the *Manchester Union Leader* received another letter containing a confession from someone saying he received $1,000 to assist with the fake "Canuck hoax." Segretti often paid his operatives for individual acts. Segretti admitted he paid both Bob Benz and Doug Kelly thousands of dollars for aiding him with dirty tricks and both of them lived in Florida. The fact that Segretti paid Kelly almost exactly $1,000 more than he dished out to Benz points to Kelly as the possible author of the Canuck Letter.

Again, there is no direct proof that the Canuck Letter was one of the dirty tricks perpetrated upon Muskie by Segretti. Segretti said he "no idea" who had sent it, but he conceded to this author that the Canuck Letter was a fake. Additionally, Segretti refused to rule out the possibility that one of his agents in Florida produced the document and mailed it to New Hampshire.

9. Florida

Donald Segretti's most comprehensive dirty tricks activity took place in Florida. This chapter looks at the Segretti operation in the Sunshine State. It also includes a partial list of pranks, black advance operations, and dirty tricks Segretti and his associates played in the Sunshine State.

Florida was important to the Nixon campaign from very early on. Pat Buchanan related to John Mitchell and H. R. Haldeman on January 2, 1972 "clearly, the Florida primary is shaping up as the first good opportunity and perhaps the last good opportunity to derail the Muskie candidacy."

Segretti began his operation in Florida by recruiting Bob Benz, the twenty-five year-old President of the Tampa Young Republicans Club, to lead the operation there. Segretti also hired Doug Kelly, also a leader of the Young Republican club, to handle dirty tricks in the Miami area.

Segretti said he contacted Benz "quite by accident, really." Segretti said, "When I arrived in Tampa, I called a local Republican office and asked if he knew of any individual that might like to do some part time work and I was given the name of Mr. Benz."

As for hiring Kelly, Segretti said, "Mr. Kelly's name I received from Mr. Benz and I received it from another individual when I went to Miami, whose name I got from the White

House advance list. The name of Kelly came up both times, so I subsequently called Mr. Kelly."

According to Segretti, Benz and Kelly "expressed a willingness to" take part in the operation. In addition, both appeared "knowledgeable about the inner workings of a political campaign."

Segretti had learned his lesson in New Hampshire. He did not provide his operatives with his real name. In fact, they did not learn his identity until months later, when they and Segretti were in deep trouble.

Segretti paid his operatives well for their work. Before their pranks ended, Benz received $2,417 for his efforts, while Segretti doled $3,426 out to Kelly. As stated earlier, the fact that Kelly received almost exactly $1,000 more than Benz did suggests that Kelly may have been responsible for the Canuck Letter.

During their first meeting, Segretti instructed Benz "to obtain hecklers, pickets, and also to get people to infiltrate into the campaigns to gather information." Segretti promised to provide the funds necessary to pay the individuals Benz brought into the scheme.

Benz wasted no time in recruiting Peg Griffin, a secretary living in Tampa. Griffin was active in Republican politics, and she was anxious to help. When Benz asked her to infiltrate the Muskie campaign, she agreed immediately. Benz told the Muskie people that Griffin "was a Republican, that she did not care for the President's policies, and she was a backer of Senator Muskie." The Muskie "people" bought the cover story Benz gave them about Griffin and put her to work at the Senator's Tampa headquarters.

Griffin proved more than worth the $75 weekly salary Benz paid her. Griffin provided Benz with a wealth of Muskie campaign literature, information regarding Muskie campaign strategy, stationary bearing Muskie's campaign letterhead, and the names of some of Muskie's financial contributors. Benz mailed copies of everything he received from Griffin to Segretti's post office box in California. Segretti and Benz applied a large portion of the intelligence Griffin provided them in the development and execution of Segretti's dirty tricks operation in the Sunshine State.

Griffin also succeeded in disturbing the Muskie campaign in her own right. In early 1972, Griffin learned that Muskie planned a secret $1,000-a-plate fundraising dinner following a public reception. Only 17 rich donors were to attend the fundraiser. Griffin added the information about the fundraiser on the bottom two lines of a Muskie press release announcing the public reception.

Of course, when the press learned of Muskie's intention to cater to 17 rich "fat cats," it caused a stir. The Muskie campaign reacted to the bad press it received by cancelling the fundraiser altogether. However, it was too late to repair the damage to the Muskie campaign.

Griffin's little dirty trick certainly cost Muskie the considerable sum of $17,000 (more than $100,000 in today's currency) immediately, and more down the line in lost campaign donations. The revelation that Muskie was holding a private fundraiser also dented the Senator's well-cultivated image as a "man of the people." and likely cost him a considerable amount of working-class support.

Benz also recruited Eselene Frolich to infiltrate the Florida campaign of Washington Senator Henry "Scoop" Jackson. Frolich provided Benz and Segretti with the same kinds of information on Jackson that Griffin provided on Muskie. Frolich's intelligence gathering provided very valuable to Benz and he used it to devise several dirty tricks against Jackson.

Doug Kelly gave Segretti the impression that he had planted two individuals in the Muskie campaign in Miami, but this proved not to be true. Kelly had no operatives working inside the Miami headquarters. It is still uncertain where Kelly got the information he claimed that came from the nonexistent agents he supposedly planted in Miami. It is possible that he simply invented it.

Segretti spread more false and misleading literature in Florida than he did in any other state – all of it illegal. In Florida and elsewhere, all the false and misleading literature generated and disseminated by Segretti was illegal due to the simple fact that it did not carry a statement confirming that the Committee to Reelect the President financed it.

Segretti caused the printing and distributing of about 300 posters that read, "Help Muskie Support Bussing (sic) More Children Now." Segretti, Benz, and Kelly distributed 100 to 125 of the posters in the Miami and Tampa areas.

Of course, the intent of the posters was to tie Muskie to the very unpopular policy of busing schoolchildren across district lines to achieve racial integration. The busing poster carried the signature of the "Mothers Backing Muskie Committee." There was no such group. Segretti created the name.

Segretti had about 1,000 4-inch-by-6-inch cards printed for Benz and his agents to distribute at a Tampa rally for Alabama Governor George Wallace. On one side the cards read, "If You Liked Hitler, You'll Just Love Wallace." On the reverse side they read, A Vote for Wallace is a Wasted Vote. On March 14, cast your vote for Senator Edmund Muskie." Of course, the intent of the cards was to drive Wallace supporters away from Muskie permanently.

Peg Griffin purloined a stash of the stationary from Muskie headquarters and Donald Segretti put it to nefarious use. On February 25, 1972, Segretti sent a letter on the stolen Muskie campaign stationary to Senator Henry Jackson's Florida campaign manager and a select few of America's top syndicated political commentators. The letter alleged that the Muskie campaign was using government typewriters illegally. It continued that government employees manned the typewriters and worked for the Muskie campaign at taxpayer expense. Segretti and his minions also sent copies of the letter to Jackson's headquarters in Tampa, and Washington, D.C.

The phony typewriter letter cost Muskie no lasting damage. However, it was an issue for a day.

In March 1972, the Florida primary was fast approaching and Segretti wanted to make a big splash before the Democrats went to the polls. One evening, Segretti downed a few beers with his cohorts, and in his buzzed state, had a sinister idea. Segretti conceived a letter, the contents of which were vile even by the standards of most dirty tricks artists. Segretti wrote a counterfeit letter on some of the stolen Muskie stationary. Then he mailed it to Benz.

The letter alleged that Senator Henry Jackson had fathered a child with a girl of the tender age of seventeen. It also claimed that the police arrested Jackson while he was engaging in homosexual acts.

The letter impugned the character of Senator Hubert Humphrey, as well. It falsely stated that the District of Columbia police had charged Humphrey with a DUI while the Senator was in the company of prostitutes that Washington lobbyists had procured for him.

Later, Segretti contended that it was not his desire to have anyone believe the contents of the letter. He said he just wanted to create confusion among the candidates. However, it is difficult to believe that he did not intend to smear the reputations of Senators Jackson and Humphrey.

Segretti instructed Benz to print 20 to 40 copies of the letter and have them distributed. Benz passed the fake material to one of his recruits, George Hearing. Hearing acquired a list of Jackson supporters from Benz and mailed the letters to several of them. Benz had acquired the list earlier from Eselene Frohlich. As noted above, Frohlich was working undercover in the Jackson campaign.

The scurrilous letter slandering Jackson and Humphrey won high praise from Chaplin. Chapin chortled over the fact that the letter cost only about $20 to produce, copy, print, and mail, yet resulted in $10,000 to $20,000 worth of benefit to the Nixon campaign.

Segretti's Apology

On October 3, 1973, Donald Segretti testified before the Senate's Select Committee on Presidential Campaign Activities. Segretti said he felt remorse for the letter slandering Humphrey and Jackson, and during his opening statement, Segretti apologized for the letter. Below is Segretti's complete apology verbatim:

"I would like to make clear that this letter was my idea and was not suggested by any other person. I assume full responsibility for its contents. Each and every allegation in the letter was untrue and without any basis in fact. It was not my desire to have anyone believe the letter, but instead it was intended to create confusion among the various candidates. It is my belief that from 20 to 40 such letters were sent out, mainly to Senator Jackson's supporters. I deeply regret that I initiated this incident and wish to apologize publicly for this stupid act. I can only hope that this apology will in some way rectify the harm done to these Senators and their families."

Neither Jackson, nor Humphrey accepted Segretti's apology. Both thought it was nothing more than a self-serving attempt by Segretti to seem less odious. Many, many others shared the view of the Senators.

Below is a list of just some of the other dirty tricks Segretti and his team played in Florida.

Doug Kelly distributed a large number of fake pamphlets inviting Democratic voters to a free luncheon at the Muskie campaign headquarters in Miami. The pamphlets also promised attendees free liquor and an opportunity to meet Senator Muskie and his wife Jane. Segretti's agents placed the pamphlets in conspicuous places throughout the Miami area. In addition, Kelly put a small number at the Miami headquarters of Democratic presidential hopeful, New York Mayor John Lindsay.

The morning before the stated time of the phony luncheon, Kelly telephoned the Miami Muskie headquarters and accused Lindsay operatives of creating and distributing the invitations. Even though the Muskie campaign was now aware of the invitations announcing the nonexistent lunch, it was too late to let everyone with an invitation know it was all just a prank and a number of people did show up for the event.

The fake invitations served their primary purpose of causing confusion within the Muskie camp and to embarrassing Senator Muskie. Secondarily, Segretti's operatives desired to drive a wedge between Senator Muskie and Mayor Lindsay in the hopes that they would not work together in the fall campaign. Of course, since neither man won the nomination the secondary purpose never came into play.

Later, Segretti and Kelly obtained an actual invitation to a Muskie campaign event in Miami. They added a line to the invitation that read, "Free Food and Alcoholic Beverages Provided." Then they distributed the doctored invitations across the greater Miami area and caused more embarrassment for the Muskie campaign.

Doug Kelly sent out "three of four" bogus press releases on Muskie stationary in Miami. The press releases misrepresented Muskie's positions on such issues as his support for Israel and school busing. In addition, the press releases brought attention to former Vice President Humphrey's positions those issues. The press releases followed Segretti's basic plan to turn voters away from Muskie and "Dividing the Democrats."

Kelly distributed flyers announcing a speech by former Secretary of Interior Stewart Udall that the Florida Young Democrats had already cancelled. The flyers caused a great deal of confusion and the Young Democrats felt compelled to reschedule the Udall event.

Kelly handed out fliers in Miami, falsely attributed to the Lindsay campaign, attacking Senator Muskie's position on Israel. The fliers claimed that Muskie favored treating Israel and Cuba the same. This, of course, antagonized both the Cuban and Jewish communities in Miami.

Kelly displayed a complete disregard for the sensibilities of the Jewish community when he placed the fake flyers under automobile windshield wipers in synagogue parking lots in the Miami Beach area.

Doug Kelly placed an advertisement with a Miami radio station contending that Senator Muskie believed in the right of self-determination for all people, and therefore the Senator supported the Castro government in Cuba. When placing the ad, Kelly represented himself as a member of Muskie's Florida staff and no one challenged him. Kelly hoped the ad would help drive members of Miami's large Cuban-American community away from Muskie.

Segretti agents also placed an ad in a Cuban-American newspaper called *Replica*. The text of the ad read:

"Muskie believes all people have a right to choose any type of government they want. The Cuban people are no exception and the United

States should not interfere. If elected, Muskie will attempt to ease tensions between the United States and Cuba. He was born in Maine and is a good American. Vote for Ed Muskie."

Again, the intent of this advertisement was to estrange Cuban-Americans from Muskie. The evidence indicates that Segretti's efforts did cause a large segment Cuban-American to mistrust Muskie.

Operatives of the Segretti dirty tricks team placed several advertisements in Miami newspapers drawing attention to Muskie's statement that he did not think the American people were ready for an African-American vice presidential nominee. Two notable ads appeared in the *Miami Sunday Sun-Reporter*. One of them asked, "Senator Muskie. You wouldn't accept a black or American Indian, would you accept a Jewish running mate?"

As with most other aspects of the Segretti operation, its most effective use of demonstrators took place in Florida. Bob Benz recruited Kip Edwards, Al Reece, George Hearing, an older individual known only as "Duke" to organize demonstrations against Senators Muskie and Jackson in the greater Tampa area. Intelligence provided by the Segretti spies, Frohlich in the Jackson campaign, and Griffin in the Muskie campaign, was very valuable. The intelligence passed on by the Segretti moles allowed Benz to deploy demonstrators rapidly and efficiently.

Benz succeeded often in getting media coverage of the phony demonstrations he organized. This coverage only added to the distrust that developed between the various Democratic candidates. Below are descriptions of some of the demonstrations Segretti's top prankster organized.

Benz learned that Senator Jackson was speaking at the opening of his Tampa headquarters in January 1972. Benz hired a "Mr. Yancy" and Kip Edwards to stand across the street from the headquarters with signs reading, "Believe in Muskie." However, Jackson handled the situation well. Senator Jackson walked across the street and offered the demonstrators each a glass of Florida orange juice. Newspapers across the state carried the photo of Jackson smiling broadly and displaying his generosity to the protesters. As silly as it was, the incident cost Musky at least a little credibility.

Peg Griffin also made Benz privy to Muskie's schedule as the Senator whistle-stopped his way around the Sunshine State in a red, white, and blue train. Benz arranged sign welding protesters to demonstrate at Muskie's stop at Winter Haven. The protesters, displaying as much anger as they could muster, shook signs bearing large letters that spelled out "WALLACE COUNTRY" at the Maine Senator. The aforementioned George Hearing, Kip Edwards, and Duke demonstrated against Muskie at this event.

It was about this time that Benz gained knowledge that Duke was a member of the Nazi Party and that he was a former Strom Trooper in Hitler's Germany. This knowledge did not cause Benz to rid the organization.

Kelly also took advantage of his access to Muskie's schedule. On several occasions, Kelly called individuals, especially members of the press, and changed appointment times they had to meet with the Senator for personal interviews, etc. Of course, Muskie had no idea that Kelly changed the appointments to other times, or cancelled them altogether. This dirt trick caused the Muskie campaign problems, especially with various media outlets that missed deadlines because of Kelly's dirty trick.

Benz and Hearing discussed how to improve their disruption of the Muskie campaign several times. On one instance, they decided to furnish false information to Muskie campaign headquarters and to the public regarding Muskie's train schedule. To this end, they placed false advertisements in some Florida newspapers listing wrong times for the arrival of the Muskie train in selected towns and cities. At the very least, these ads caused confusion among those wishing to see and hear Muskie and it made the Senator's campaign appear incompetent.

Benz arranged for several demonstrators to protest at a Muskie rally at the University of Southern Florida. At this rally, Benz and his partners passed out newspaper reprints critical of Senator Muskie.

Benz organized many other demonstrations at Muskie appearances in Tampa. On one occasion, he arranged for the protest of a Muskie rally by African-Americans. Benz provided a number of African-Americans with "racially related placards" criticizing Muskie's remark that America was not ready for a black vice presidential candidate.

(Note: On September 7, 1971, in a meeting in the Watts section of Los Angeles, between Muskie and black leaders, he told them that a Democratic ticket with an African-American vice presidential nominee could not win the election.)

Another time, about 10 of Segretti's agents protested at a Muskie rally. These picketers also carried signs criticizing Muskie for refusing to consider an African-American as his running mate.

One of the sillier (and funnier) dirty tricks the Segretti team pulled on Muskie took place in Gainesville, Florida. Doug Kelly gave a female student from the University of Florida a crisp new $20 bill, and in exchange, she agreed to perform a prank for him. The beautiful student stripped down naked and then ran around in front of Senator Muskie's hotel in Gainesville screaming at the top of her well-developed lungs, "Senator Muskie, I love you! Senator Muskie, I love you!" The incident got a lot of play in Gainesville newspapers.

Two students working for Segretti protested the opening of Senator Jackson's campaign headquarters in Tampa. The demonstrators carried signs reading "Muskie for President." This action was more likely to harm Muskie than Jackson, but it could not have done Jackson any good either.

Shortly before the Florida primary, Senator Muskie held a press conference at Miami's Four Ambassadors Hotel. Kelly recruited a number of the persons of Cuban extraction to protest at the press conference. Kelly provided the protesters with signs reading "Muskie Go Home" and "We Want a Free Cuba!"

In addition to the signs, Kelly provided the demonstrators with large Humphrey campaign pins to wear. When a Muskie aide inquired regarding the identity of the demonstrators, Kelly whispered to him "confidentially" that the protesters were employees of Senator Jackson.

Thus, Kelly was able through his phony demonstration to connect Muskie to an unpopular cause in Florida, and to generate anger in the Muskie camp at Senators Humphrey and Jackson.

At the same event, Kelly pulled two large white mice from under the long overcoat he was wearing and dropped them on the floor. Kelly had tied a ribbon to the tail of each of the mice reading, "Muskie is a Rat Fink." Kelly was not finished. He released a small finch and watched it fly all around the room. The mice and little bird caused a great deal of commotion and disrupted the press conference for several minutes.

On at least four occasions during the Florida primary campaign cycle, Segretti's agents employed "stink bombs" to harass Muskie, his staff, and his supporters. Doug Kelly convinced a chemist friend of his to create the stink bombs for him. The substance the chemist used to create the bomb was butyl mercaptan. Butyl mercaptan is a clear to yellowish liquid with an extremely foul-smell, commonly described as "skunk" odor. Butyl mercaptan is noxious and caustic, and at sufficiently high concentrations, it produces serious health effects in both humans and animals. However, applied in the way Segretti and Kelly intended, it was physically harmless.

Despite what Segretti and his associates called them, the stink bombs did not explode, they gave off no heat, or even smoke. The butyl mercaptan mixture simply gave off a powerfully foul skunk-like odor when released into the air.

Shortly before the Florida primary, Senator Muskie scheduled a picnic in the Miami area. Segretti and Kelly took the butyl mercaptan mixture, placed it in a Coca-Cola bottle, and sealed the bottle with candle wax. The two pranksters took the bottle to the picnic and while in the midst of the crowd, Segretti slammed the bottle against the ground, breaking it and releasing the skunk odor into the air.

The stink bomb did not have the desired effect of causing the crowd to scatter, but Kelly later said, "Everybody thought that the food was bad, so it kind of made the picnic a bad affair."

Relatively pleased with the results of their first stink bomb attack, Segretti and his flunkies attempted others. After the Muskie picnic, Segretti sauntered north to Tampa with three vials of his stink bomb liquid. Segretti gave the vials to Robert Benz and ordered him to use them against Muskie.

Benz decided to utilize one of the stink bombs at a Muskie picnic in Tampa. Benz then passed the other two stink bombs to George Hearing. Hearing set the two stink bombs off in the Muskie headquarters in Tampa on the day before the Florida primary (March 3, 1972).

Hearing placed one of the stink bombs through a hole in the window in the offices housing Senator Muskie's campaign phone bank.

Hearing set the other stink bomb off in the main Muskie headquarters. In order to get the stink bomb inside the headquarters, Hearing pried off a window screen, opened the window, and threw the stink bomb inside. By Florida law, the act of breaking into the headquarters constituted burglary. Even Donald Segretti conceded that Hearing's act constituted "unauthorized entry."

The stink bombs set off on primary eve disrupted, confused, and interfered with the Muskie operation and likely cost the Senator a handful of votes.

Both Kelly and Benz placed one Democratic candidate's sticker on another candidate's posters and literature. This simple act caused bad feelings among the respective Democratic campaigns.

Kelly also made efforts to tie up Muskie phone banks on the day of the Florida primary. Kelly hoped he could disrupt the Muskie effort to get out the vote and other activities the Senator's campaign had planned for the day. Kelly dialed the numbers used by the Muskie campaign from pay phones, (campaigns didn't phone banks with hundreds of numbers in those days). When a Muskie campaign worker answered the phone, Kelly just dropped the receiver, leaving it off the hook. He then placed an "Out of Order" on the outside of the phone booth in an effort to keep the Muskie phone line tied up all day. This dirty trick did not work. Kelly did not know that in a short time, the phone company automatically ended the connections.

On primary day in Florida, Segretti and Kelly had flowers, chicken, and between $300 and $400 worth of liquor sent to the Muskie headquarters in Miami, and had the items charged to the Senator's campaign.

Most of the dirty tricks in Florida targeted Muskie for the benefit of McGovern. However, Kelly did slam McGovern a few times as well. Kelly distributed a one-page flier in the Miami area titled, "George McGovern's Real Record on the War." The flier presented, in chronological order, McGovern's votes on selected matters brought before the Senate relating to the war in Vietnam. At the bottom of the flier, it stated, "Don't believe it. Check the record. Prepared by Students for Honesty in Government." The Students for Honesty in Government was still another bogus organization invented by Segretti.

Kelly thought it would be funny to have Senator McGovern sign the flier. At an outdoor McGovern campaign event, Kelly folded a flier over so none of the print was visible, and then he pushed through the crowd to the Senator and asked for an autograph. The ever-obliging McGovern smiled and signed the paper. When Kelly showed the autographed flier to his fellow pranksters, they all shared a wicked laugh.

The results of the Florida primary were good news for the White House. Alabama Governor Wallace won Florida with 41.6% of vote. Humphrey finished second with 18.6%. Jackson was third with 13.5%. Muskie limped in 8.9% and a fourth place finish.

Muskie did so poorly in Florida that his campaign was on virtual life-support coming out of the Sunshine State. He needed a miracle now. Segretti's operation had done its job in Florida as well as it could.

10. Illinois

Segretti recruited Tom Visney and Charles Svihlik to perform dirty tricks in Illinois. Segretti mailed Visney, between 500 and 1,000 copies of a pamphlet drafted in the White House by presidential speechwriters Ken Khachigian and Pat Buchanan. The original pamphlet carried the signature of the phony "Citizens for a Liberal Alternative." The pamphlet presented a photograph of Senator Muskie smoking a large cigar. The caption stated that Muskie was no different from "the Nixons, Agnews, Michells, Connallys we have now." Visney distributed most of the pamphlets in the Chicago area.

Also in Chicago, Tom Visney placed an anti-Muskie advertisement in a local newspaper and on several radio stations. The ads supported the candidacy of Minnesota Senator Eugene McCarthy. The ads were tough on Muskie, contending that the Senator from Maine possessed neither the emotional stability, nor the requisite experience to hold the office of President.

Segretti caused the distribution of some of the "Help Muskie Support Bussing (sic) More Children Now" posters in the Chicago area.

Segretti hoped his dirty tricks in Illinois would hurt Muskie and to help propel McCarthy back into the presidential race.

Segretti's dirty tricks failed in Illinois. Muskie won easily with 62.6% of the vote while

McCarthy only received 36.3%. The result knocked McCarthy out of the presidential sweepstakes, but Muskie's victory gave him no momentum and he still faced a life or death contest in Wisconsin two weeks later. Of course, Segretti was working to defeat Muskie in the Badger State.

11. Wisconsin

Tom Visney and Charles Svihlik also operated in Wisconsin for Segretti doing the same sort of things they did in Illinois. However, with Muskie on the ropes, Segretti wanted to land a knockout blow in Wisconsin. Segretti decided to go to Wisconsin himself and spring a few pranks before the Democratic presidential preference primary on April 4.

Segretti and Benz drove from Florida to Wisconsin in late March 1972. However, their target was not Muskie, but Humphrey. This shift in dirty tricks reflected the opinion of the White House that Humphrey was now Nixon's most dangerous opponent.

After arriving in Milwaukee, Segretti and Benz distributed fake invitations for a free "All You Can Eat" lunch on April Fools' Day at the Hubert Humphrey headquarters. The invitation also stated that Humphrey would provide free beer and other alcoholic beverages during the event. In addition, the invitations promised that guests would have the opportunity to meet Senator Humphrey, actor Lorne Greene, and the wife of the late Reverend Martin Luther King, Coretta Scott King.

The purpose of the invitations was to disrupt the Humphrey campaign, but Segretti wanted to add to the chagrin the invitations caused by creating increased hard feelings between the Democratic candidates. He called local media outlets and told them that Muskie supporters were responsible for the phony invitations.

Segretti and Benz also distributed bumper stickers containing derogatory and sexually charged slogans directed against Muskie. The purpose of these despicable bumper stickers was to repulse potential Muskie voters and to cause them to vote for others.

On primary day in Wisconsin (April 4, 1972), Segretti and Benz ordered flowers, chicken, and pizza sent to Muskie's hotel room and charged the items to the Senator. In addition, the pranksters ordered two limousines sent to Muskie's hotel, again, at his expense.

The primary results were McGovern 29.6%, Wallace 22.0%, Humphrey 20.7%, Muskie 10.3%, and others 17.4%.

Adding insult to the injury of Muskie's loss in the Wisconsin primary, the fake orders for food and drink Segretti and Benz placed caused anger, confusion, and no little amount of embarrassment among Muskie and his staff.

President Nixon expressed elation at the result of the Wisconsin primary. The voters of the Badger State ended any hope that Muskie would recover and win the nomination. Muskie continued on, but he was finished. On the other hand, the candidate the White House feared the least was now the frontrunner. Senator George McGovern of South Dakota sat atop of the rubble of the party of Andrew Jackson and Franklin Delano Roosevelt. Nixon could not have been happier.

12. Pennsylvania

Segretti and his henchmen began their dirty tricks operation in Pennsylvania focused, as they were elsewhere, on damaging Senator Muskie. However, after the Wisconsin primary, Segretti and his pranksters, as did everyone in the United States, knew Muskie was no longer viable. Thus, they switched their emphasis and pointed their dirty tricks more at Humphrey than Muskie. They felt the ideal scenario would be for Alabama Governor George Wallace to win the primary.

Bob Benz travelled to Pennsylvania to recruit individuals to infiltrate the various primary campaigns there. However, he had less success in Pennsylvania than he did in Florida.

Seeing Pennsylvania as an important primary state, Segretti decided to continue the recruitment effort on his own. He located Skip Zimmer and Bob Nieley and hired them to work for him in the Keystone State. Segretti instructed Zimmer and Nieley to pass anti-Muskie literature at the Senator's appearances and to organize demonstrations at Muskie rallies.

Zimmer took pride in his work. He sent clippings from the *Pennsylvania Voice* on April 19, 1972 to Segretti. The clippings detailed hecklers and protestors being nuisances at Muskie rallies. The clippings provided proof positive the dirty tricks campaign was succeeding in Pennsylvania.

Zimmer also hired individuals to attend Muskie rallies bearing signs inscribed with such slogans as "M-U-S-K-I-E spells Loser" and "HHH is the Man."

Another poster stated, "Muskie: Florida, 9 percent; Wisconsin, 10 percent; Pennsylvania 11 percent (with luck)".

Still another posted stated, "probusing Ed's children go to private school".

After one Muskie rally, somewhat satisfied with his dirty tricks, Zimmer commented on his effort in a letter to Segretti. "Though the press was disappointing . . . We did greatly piss off [Muskie's] staff and rattle him considerably". Zimmer was commenting on the fact that "Muskie looked right up at these . . . [posters] right in front of him as he left, and scowled perceptibly."

Zimmer arranged for protesters at Muskie rallies to post with signs saying, "Gays for Muskie."

Although Bob Nieley always denied he ever did more than collect and then pass on campaign literature to Segretti, the evidence shows otherwise.

Nieley and Zimmer concentrated on having hecklers at as many Democratic candidates' rallies in Pennsylvania as possible. After their hecklers disrupted a Humphrey rally in Philadelphia, Zimmer called the Humphrey headquarters and talked to Jack Cannon, Senator Humphrey's Deputy Press Secretary. Zimmer told Cannon that Muskie staffers had paid the hecklers $100 each to cause the disturbance and Cannon believed him.

One of Segretti's friends in Philadelphia took advantage of Democratic workers at a Humphrey rally there. Segretti's friend had between 50 and 70 fliers printed. The fliers carried large print reading "Trust Muskie" or "Trust Senator Muskie." The individual had the Democratic workers pass out the fliers at the rally.

Muskie's most sincere supporters held out faint hope that the Senator could pull off a big victory in Pennsylvania and revive his fortunes, but it was not to be. Muskie finished fourth in the primary and he was fast becoming an afterthought.

The Segretti operation did not do as well in Pennsylvania as it had elsewhere. Humphrey won rather handily with 35.1% of the vote, to 21.3% for Wallace, and 20.4% for McGovern. Muskie was far back.

13. Indiana and Tennessee

Tom Visney and Charles Svihlik operated in Indiana doing the same sort of things they did in other states.

Early in the contest, the somewhat conservative Hoosier State looked like a good place to try to stop Muskie. However, by the time the primary rolled around, Indiana was a contest between Humphrey and Wallace. Yet, the few and mild dirty tricks performed there stood to help broaden the wedge in the various factions of the Democratic Party.

Segretti caused some of the posters that read, "Help Muskie Support Bussing (sic) More Children Now" sent to Indiana. The number of posters distributed is unknown.

The Nixon camp hoped for a Wallace win in Indiana, but the results disappointed them. Humphrey won a narrow victory in the Hoosier State.

Segretti attempted to gain knowledge about the Muskie effort in Tennessee, but nothing came of it. It didn't matter anyway. By the time the Tennessee Democrats went to the polls, Muskie was finished and Wallace ran roughshod over the field in the Volunteer State.

14. California

Segretti recruited several agents for the California Democratic primary. One of them was James Robert "Bob" Norton. Norton set up an answering service (remember, this was in the days before cell phones and other instant communications systems) for Segretti in St. Louis. The service could handle calls from anywhere in the United States. In addition, Norton brought in a number of others with deep experience in California politics. Segretti relied on these individuals to distribute phony literature and to protest during appearances by Democratic presidential candidates in Los Angeles.

In his meeting with Dwight Chapin in early November 1971, Segretti became aware that Senator Muskie would visit the Los Angeles area around November 6. Chapin ordered Segretti to hire a number of demonstrators and hecklers to protest Muskie's visit. In addition, Chapin ordered Segretti to learn the schedules of Muskie and his staff.

Segretti hired a private investigator named Jess Burdick to help him. Burdick had worked previously as an investigator for the United States Army's Criminal Investigations Division. Burdick tailed Muskie for the weekend the Senator was in Los Angeles. Burdick made a list of the license plate numbers used by Muskie's campaign but did little else.

Burdick shocked Segretti when he presented the dirty tricks artist with the skimpy, mostly worthless information and a bill for $325. Segretti thought the charge was much too steep for the service rendered, but he paid it. However, Segretti never used Burdick again.

After Dwight Chapman informed him that Senator Muskie would speak at Nixon's alma mater, Whittier College, In November 1971, Segretti ordered the printing of a large number of lists of "hard questions" for Muskie. Segretti then had the lists passed out to students at the Muskie rally.

One of the questions Segretti gave to the students was, "Do you refuse to even consider a black or Chicano as your running mate?"

In anticipation to Muskie's answer to the question above, the questioner was to state, "Your public answer that they do not yet have political equality only fosters any bias that exists and avoids the question."

Another question Segretti proposed was, "Why do you speak in terms of equality for minorities, yet send your children to all-white private schools?"

One of the students asked Muskie a loaded question about the Senator's stance that he favored abortions for "therapeutic reasons." The question came from Segretti's list. Dwight Chapin praised Segretti for that question.

Segretti had good success recruiting infiltrators for the Democratic primary in California. In Los Angeles, Segretti had a conversation with an old high school friend of Dwight Chapin's named Ward Turnquist.

Turnquist then contacted a man named Pat O'Brien and recruited him to infiltrate Muskie's campaign in the Los Angeles area and gather what intelligence he could. O'Brien went undercover in the Muskie campaign in December 1971 and worked as a spy for Segretti until April 1972.

Bob Norton hired Mike Silva to work in the San Francisco area and acquire information about Muskie for Segretti. Silva told Segretti that he had planted two spies in the Muskie campaign in late February 1972, but that was not true. Silva did not plant anyone in the Muskie campaign. He merely gathered campaign literature he picked up from a Political Science course at San Francisco State University and forwarded it to Segretti's Los Angeles post office box. Silva's subterfuge succeeded. Segretti paid for the material and did not learn that Silva had scammed him until much later.

Several months before the California primary, Segretti reprinted a newspaper advertisement taken out in New York papers by Stewart Mott and the "Committee for Honesty in Politics." The heading of the ad was "Disgusting, the Secret Money in Presidential Politics." The original ad made a reference to Senator Muskie's alleged failure to make a full disclosure of his campaign finances.

At the bottom of the reprint, Segretti added the note, "Now he says he will disclose the fat cats behind him (after he lost badly in Florida and cried in New Hampshire). Why is he waiting for full disclosure – is it time to fix his books? The committee will look for your name as part of Muskie's fat cats! They better be there!"

Segretti's lackeys handed out copies of the doctored reprint to individuals entering a Muskie fundraiser.

While the distorted reprint carried direct threats, Segretti said he didn't intend to frighten anyone. Segretti said, "The purpose of that language was to irritate people rather than to actually frighten or threaten anyone."

From even before the New Hampshire primary, the rigors of running for President had caused the large field of Democratic hopefuls in 1972 to narrow. By the time the June 6, California Democratic primary drew near, only two serious Democratic contenders for the nomination remained standing, Senators George McGovern and Hubert Humphrey. However, a few others could not admit defeat and they continued their futile efforts to gain the nomination. This situation presented opportunities to Segretti.

Most, but not all, of the false and misleading literature Segretti pumped into California attacked one of the two remaining candidates and was attributed to the other. By doing this, Segretti believed he could keep the leading Democrats at each other's throats until the Democratic national convention, and beyond.

Joe Arriola, the Miami printer E. Howard Hunt ordered Segretti to use, produced the majority of the fake materials Segretti distributed in his dirty trick operation.

In their effort to disrupt the Democratic primary in California, Segretti and his band of pranksters issued ever more insidious and disquieting literature. A few examples are below:

Segretti's most vile expression of political cynicism is almost unbelievable, even after all these years. Below are the details:

Segretti issued a press release on Humphrey stationary "For Immediate Release." The press release made the outrageous and utterly false claims regarding Shirley Chisholm, a member of Congress from New York and the first African-American woman to make a serious run at a major party presidential nomination.

The press release stated that Representative Chisholm was committed to a private home for the mentally ill in February 1951 and remained confined there until April 1952. The letter further claimed that Chisholm was still under psychiatric care. It also described the "alleged" behaviors of Chisholm including: that she was a "transvestite" and that she was hostile and aggressive towards everyone she encountered. The press release further claimed that Chisholm's psychiatrist wrote that she "makes facial grimaces, and gesters (sic) to herself, exhibits inexplicable laughter and weeping, and at times has an abnormal interest in urine and feces which she smears on walls and herself."

Segretti tried to reinforce the idea that the phony press release came from the Humphrey campaign. He included HHH at the bottom of the press release.

According to Segretti, he did not intend anyone to believe the allegations made against Representative Chisholm. He said he desired to harm Humphrey by causing voters to believe that former Vice President Humphrey's staff distributed the press release. However, he does not regret the harm he could have done to Chisholm and her family.

Segretti sent the fake press release to between ten and fifteen California newspapers. Most of the readers of these papers were African-Americans. He also sent a copy of the press release to Dwight Chapin. According to Segretti, Chapin "laughed for a period of time" when he read the scurrilous press release.

Segretti mailed out two other bogus press releases on Humphrey stationary. One stated that former President Johnson favored Senator Humphrey for the Democratic presidential nomination (which was true, but damaging to Humphrey nonetheless). The other press release distorted Humphrey's position on a California ballot initiative in 1972.

Segretti caused the printing and distribution of bumper stickers that read, "Humphrey, he started the war, don't give him another chance." The bulk of 1,000 or so of the bumper stickers produced found their way to voters in California, but a few went elsewhere, including about 75 that went directly to Humphrey delegates.

The bumper stickers carried the sign of a nonexistent organization called "Democrats for a Peace Candidate." Segretti invented the name.

Segretti fashioned and distributed another pamphlet for the California primary modeled after the one created by Khachigian and Buchanan that he used in Illinois. He added the signature of the phony "Citizens for a Liberal Alterative" to this pamphlet as well. This silly pamphlet portrayed a photo of a smiling Senator Humphrey holding a large billfish. The caption read, "Humphrey: A fishy smell for the White House."

Segretti distributed about 5,000 of the pamphlets in San Francisco, Los Angeles, and throughout Orange County. Segretti believed that the pamphlets would deepen the division between the various leaders of the Democratic Party – especially Humphrey and McGovern.

Segretti was responsible for the preparation and mailing of a letter over the forged signature of Barbara Barron, who was the Coordinator of Minnesota Senator Eugene McCarthy's California campaign. Segretti had the letter printed on "McCarthy 1972" stationary and sent out to McCarthy delegates urging them to switch their allegiance to Senator Humphrey.

In addition, Segretti sent another letter with slightly different wording to Representative Chisholm's supporters also bearing the forged signature of Barron. That letter urged Chisholm supporters to switch to Humphrey as well. A large percentage of those that received the letters believed it was genuine long after the Democratic national convention.

Segretti purposely mailed some of the forged letters without stamps so that the postal service would return them to McCarthy's California headquarters.

The forged Barbara Barron letters was a crime for which Segretti never faced charges. Segretti admitted that Barron's signature was forged, but he never admitted who forged it.

Segretti also sent faked letters on stationary of 1972 presidential hopeful, Los Angeles Mayor Sam Yorty to local newspapers including the *Los Angeles Free Press*. These phony letters claimed the forged letters supposedly from Barbara Barron actually came from the Yorty campaign.

In addition, Segretti had a full-page article inserted into the May 26, 1972, *Los Angeles Free Press* which read, "Is Mayor Yorty Involved in a Plot to Sabotage McGovern." The article contained the bogus switch vote letters described above and a letter on Mayor Yorty's campaign stationery falsely accusing the Mayor of responsibility for the switch vote letters to McCarthy delegates and Chisholm supporters. Segretti attributed the article to a young, Yorty supporter disenchanted by the letters. However, Segretti later admitted that he penned the article himself.

Segretti fooled the editors of the *Free Press*. They believed the forged letters to McCarthy delegates and Chisholm supporters were genuine and had originated with the Yorty for President Committee. Of course, by the time the *Free Press* discovered it was mistaken, it was too late to repair the damage.

The undeniable fact is that Segretti succeeded splendidly with the forged Barbara Barron letters and the fake letters placing the blame for them on Mayor Yorty. They caused anger, undermined any trust the Democratic candidates may have had for each other, and widened the gulf between the various Democratic candidates.

In November 1971, Segretti paid a friend of his from Turlock, California to arrange for a group of demonstrators with signs saying, "Kennedy for President" to line up in front of a San Francisco hotel where Senators Muskie and Humphrey were attending a Democratic fundraising dinner.

Segretti attempted to arrange for demonstrators to protest the speech by Muskie at Whittier College. The disruption of this event was evidently very important to the White House, because unbeknownst to Segretti and his band, campaign aide to President Nixon, Herbert L. "Bart" Porter, and Jeb Magruder ordered several other demonstrators carrying anti-Muskie signs to protest the event as well.

Segretti hired individuals to demonstrate outside various fundraising dinners hosted by Democratic candidates in California. One person Segretti hired was Jim Popovich. Popovich promised to put together a "flying squad" of about ten Nixon supporters. This flying squad, so promised Popovich, could deploy and demonstrate at Muskie events on very short notice. The idea intrigued Segretti and he paid Popovich $130 to organize the squad. However, Popovich could not deliver on his promises, and Segretti eventually fired him.

Segretti reworked a previously devised anti-Muskie document and transformed it into an anti-Humphrey pamphlet. Segretti took a photo of Humphrey and United Mine Workers Union President Tony Boyle and placed it over the caption "Memories of 1968 – stop the bombing – end U.S. aggression." The pamphlet continued, "Hubert H. Humphrey would be no different from the Nixons, Agnews, Mitchells, Reagans we have now. He is the boss candidate . . ." The pamphlet stated that it originated from "Democrats against Bossism, T. Wilson Chairman." The truth was that there was no such organization, nor any such person. Segretti invented both. Segretti circulated about 3,000 of the pamphlets.

When Humphrey became aware of the existence of this pamphlet, he was "quite stirred up and actually believed that Senator McGovern or Senator Muskie was" responsible for its production. Humphrey remained livid over the pamphlet for a long time.

The Nixon campaign got their wish and McGovern (43.5%) defeated Humphrey (38.6%) in the California primary and virtually wrapped up the Democratic nomination.

15. New York and Texas

Segretti wanted to do some things in the last of the Democratic primaries. Even though by the time the New York primary rolled around on June 20, 1972, it was not very meaningful as far as delegation selection was concerned, it was still important, due to its size and the media attention it drew. Segretti convinced Michael Martin, Jr. to help disrupt the New York primary. Martin infiltrated the Humphrey campaign in New York City and provided a good amount of intelligence to Segretti.

Martin won the trust of the Humphrey people in New York City so completely that he received an offer to serve as Director of Humphrey's campaign in the northern part of the state. Martin turned down the position so he could remain in New York City and continue to gather intelligence for Segretti.

Segretti enlisted Bobby Garner of Houston to help initiate dirty tricks in Texas, provided the state became critical in the Democratic Party's nominating process. Segretti paid Garner $265, some of it earmarked to pay an infiltrator of Muskie's Texas campaign. This spy was hired to gather information on the Muskie campaign in February, March, and April 1972, and then to mail it to Segretti. Texas proved not to be a real factor in the nominating process.

16. Washington, D.C.

Around April 13, 1972, Donald Segretti and Doug Kelly flew up from Miami to Washington, D.C. on the orders of E. Howard Hunt. Segretti's mission was to attempt to ruin a Muskie fundraiser scheduled for April 17.

Senator Muskie's campaign was in crisis mode. He needed a "win" to stay alive and he was out of money. On that evening, although he didn't know it at the time, Muskie held his last major fundraising dinner of the 1972 campaign. The desperate candidate chose the Washington Hilton Hotel for the vital fundraiser. E. Howard Hunt ordered Segretti to go to Washington and disrupt the event.

Following their well-developed and oft-employed dirty tricks playbook, Segretti and Kelly first handed out leaflets encouraging individuals to "protest the fat cats with signs." Then they ordered flowers, pizzas, liquor, and other items sent to the Muskie banquet and charged everything to the Muskie campaign committee. Segretti also hired a magician to perform at the event.

However, they did not stop there. Segretti and Kelly invited six ambassadors from African nations to attend the Muskie dinner. The pranksters encouraged the ambassadors to bring as many guests with them as they wished. Segretti and Kelly ordered limousines (at Muskie's expense, of course) to take the ambassadors and their guests to the Muskie event.

The result of this little dirty trick of Segretti and Kelly was that it caused confusion and greatly embarrassed Muskie and his staff. Not only did the uninvited ambassadors crash the fundraiser, but also Kelly added to the embarrassment by calling the limousine drivers back to the fundraiser several times. On each of those occasions, Kelly told the drivers that a Muskie staffer would pay them for their work. Of course, the Muskie staffer knew nothing about it and the confusion grew.

One thing that Segretti did not accomplish that evening was hiring of an elephant and having it delivered at the dinner. He tried, but there wasn't an elephant available for rent in Washington that night. His inability to find a pachyderm notwithstanding, Segretti and his agents transformed Muskie's last chance (last gasp) at saving his campaign into a disaster.

E. Howard Hunt also said that Segretti could help the President's Vietnam policy by sending supportive telegrams to the White House. The idea was that the White House would show the telegrams to the media at press conferences and build the perception that there was broad support for the President's war policies.

Segretti ordered his operatives to send as many pro-Vietnam telegrams to the White House as they could. Of course, they could not all bear the same names, so those sending the phony telegrams had to bear forged senders' names. Segretti produced two versions of the telegram containing about 200 names each (about 400 total telegrams). He made up many of the names and the rest he took from a stolen list of delegate candidates of Representative Shirley Chisholm.

17. Democratic Convention

Segretti's final meeting with E. Howard Hunt took place on June 9, 1972 at the Four Ambassadors Hotel in Miami. However, Segretti was not staying at the Four Ambassadors. He was staying at the less expensive Towne Motel a few blocks away.

Eugenio Martinez and Virgilio Gonzales, two of the "Cuban" black bag specialists Hunt and Liddy employed for break-ins and other criminal acts, also attended the meeting between Hunt and Segretti. Martinez and Gonzales were two of those arrested during the Watergate break-in on June 17.

Segretti has always held that he did not know Martinez and Gonzales, that he did not know why they attended the meeting, and that he had no prior knowledge of the Watergate burglary. In fact, even though he admitted under oath some of the details of the meeting, he now denies that it took place.

The "Cubans" may have been in Miami for more than the Watergate break-in, and the plan may have been for them to participate with Segretti in other dirty tricks at the Democratic national convention. However, Segretti refuses to shed any light on it and the author cannot prove Martinez and Gonzales had other missions beyond the Watergate burglary.

In all fairness to Segretti, there is no concrete evidence that he knew Martinez and Gonzales or that they did anything for him. It *is* strange that Segretti did not ask Hunt who Martinez and Gonzales were or why they were at the meeting. Perhaps Hunt intimidated Segretti to the degree that the dirty trickster did not dare ask any questions.

It was right in character for Hunt not to volunteer the identities of the Cubans, but it is impossible to believe that he would have allowed Martinez and Virgilio Gonzales to attend the meeting unless he had a reason for them to be there.

Since Segretti now denies that he took part in the meeting, the mystery of why Martinez and Gonzales attended may go forever unsolved.

During the meeting, Hunt ordered Segretti to find a group of demonstrators to peaceably march around in front of the Doral Hotel during the Democratic national convention (July 10-13). Hunt continued that another group of unruly and violent demonstrators (presumably hired by Liddy and Hunt) would join in with the others. Hunt's goons would then begin trying to turn the demonstration into a riot much like the one that took place at the Democratic national convention in 1968.

Hunt was certain that Senator McGovern would shoulder the blame for the mêlée. This particular dirty trick never happened. Hunt's plans for dirty tricks at the Democratic convention ended suddenly when a private security guard and officers of the Washington police department thwarted the Watergate break-in on June 17.

Segretti did schedule one dirty trick for the Democratic convention before Watergate caused his operation to fold. In May or June 1972, Segretti and Doug Kelly hired an airplane to fly over the Democratic national convention in July. They directed that the plane pull a gigantic banner stating, "PEACE, POT, PROMISCUITY. VOTE MCGOVERN." During the convention, several individuals reported seeing the plane trailing the "weird" message.

Segretti said that his operation ceased when Dwight Chapin called him shortly after the Watergate fiasco and ordered him to stop his pranks. However, by the time Segretti got the order to stop his pranks, agents of the Federal Bureau of Investigation had already contacted him. Segretti said, "I had been visited by the FBI and I think that that sobered me up a great deal." Sober or not, the FBI visit horrified him.

18. The Segretti Cover-up

In the early morning hours of June 17, 1972, police officers arrested five men during a burglary at the Watergate Hotel in Washington, D.C. The investigation of the break-in grew into a major political scandal and eventually caused the conviction of several members of the Nixon Administration and downfall of the President himself. The wide net the investigators cast ensnared Donald Segretti long before anyone knew the full extent of President Nixon's involvement in the Watergate cover-up.

The FBI first contacted Segretti by telephone very soon after the Watergate burglary. Segretti came to the attention of investigators when they came across his phone number in E. Howard Hunt's phone records. At the time, the FBI investigators didn't think Segretti was a participant in Watergate. The only interest the investigators had in Segretti was that they were tying up all loose ends. However, the call from the FBI unnerved Segretti.

Immediately after getting off the phone with the FBI, a shaken Segretti called Dwight Chapin and asked for assistance in locating a personal attorney. Chapin reassured Segretti that the FBI investigation would amount to nothing. Chapin promised to call Segretti back shortly. Chapin was lying. He understood that the Hunt-Segretti connection posed a major problem for President Nixon's reelection bid.

Despite what he told Segretti, the situation bothered Chapin. He was worried that the FBI was on the verge of discovering Segretti's dirty tricks operation. Chapin hurriedly located Gordon Strachan at the White House. After discussing the situation with Strachan, Chapin called Segretti and summoned the nervous trickster to Washington immediately.

While Chapin reestablished contact with Segretti, Strachan phoned Council to the President, John Dean. Dean had taken the lead in "managing" every aspect of the Watergate scandal for the White House. Strachan relayed that the FBI had contacted a "friend" of his named Donald Segretti. Strachan told Dean that the FBI wanted to question Segretti about his relationship with E. Howard Hunt, but not the Watergate break-in specifically. Of course, Strachan didn't know that Dean already had intimate knowledge of the Watergate incident and was leading the efforts to cover it up.

Strachan asked Dean to meet with Segretti and Dean agreed. On June 24, just a week after the Watergate break-in, Segretti, Strachan, and Dean met in the lobby of Washington's Mayflower Hotel. After a short discussion bereft of meaningful details, Dean decided that it was necessary to hold another meeting with Segretti to acquire more information. Dean ordered Segretti to come to his office the following day to continue the discussion, or as Segretti may have viewed it – the interrogation.

No one paid much attention to him the warm, sunny Sunday morning of June 25, 1972, as Segretti climbed the steps of the impressive Executive Office Building where Dean kept his office. Segretti grew tenser as he mounted each gray concrete step. The friendly security guard holding down the desk at the building's entrance had Segretti sign in on the logbook, and then Segretti made his way to Dean's office.

During their meeting, a very nervous Segretti outlined his relationship with E. Howard Hunt to Dean. Dean reassured Segretti that he had nothing to worry about concerning the FBI interview. Dean made a point of saying that the FBI didn't have any evidence against Segretti or his political espionage team. Dean continued that the FBI only wanted to do the interview because E. Howard Hunt and Segretti had been in contact via telephone.

Dean ordered Segretti with some force not to disclose the names of Chapin, Strachan, or Kalmbach, unless the FBI demanded that he reveal them. Dean did not order Segretti to lie, but he did imply that Segretti hold back as much as possible during the interview.

At the end of the meeting, Segretti felt better. He believed that Dean was acting as his attorney and that he had a good chance of surviving the whole affair without going to prison.

Segretti returned to California and sat for the FBI interview. The agents focused on Segretti's relationship with E. Howard Hunt and they did not ask him about his relationship with Chapin, Strachan, and Kalmbach. As soon as the FBI agents finished with him, Segretti telephoned John Dean and provided him with the details of the FBI interview. Dean seemed relieved.

Segretti thought his ordeal was over, but it was just beginning. In August 1972, the Watergate grand jury in Washington issued a subpoena ordering Segretti to appear and testify. Frantic, Segretti began trying to contact his friends at the White House, as well as his local attorney. Segretti finally got Dwight Chapin on the telephone. Chapin was at Miami Beach, Florida doing prep work for the Republican national convention. Segretti told Chapin about the subpoena.

Chapin had concerns that the Segretti testimony might cause problems for the President and all those involved with the various dirty tricks campaigns. Chapin called John Dean, who was also at the convention. Chapin related to Dean that Segretti was in an agitated state because of the subpoena to testify before the Watergate grand jury. Dean told Chapin that he would happily meet with Segretti in Florida, but that it was impossible for him to return to his Washington office before the conclusion of the Republican national convention.

After speaking to Chapin, Dean called Assistant Attorney General, Henry Petersen, at the Justice Department. Dean explained the "sensitive" problem confronting Segretti to Petersen. Dean told Petersen matter-of-factly that Segretti had no connection to Watergate, but that Segretti had met with E. Howard Hunt in connection with some other campaign activities. Dean explained that Segretti performed these activities at the behest of the White House.

Dean also related that Chapin and Strachan had hired Segretti and that Kalmbach had paid him. Dean then told Petersen that if Segretti's relationships with Chapin, Strachan, and Kalmbach got out, it would cause the President problems during the concluding weeks of the 1972 campaign.

The Assistant Attorney General listened quietly to John Dean's longwinded speech. When Dean finished, Petersen made it known (indirectly) that he was sympathetic to the President's plight. Petersen did not promise outright to cover-up the Segretti connection to the White House. However, he told Dean that he would see what he could do. Later, in a second conversation with Dean, Petersen related that he didn't think the Watergate prosecutors would get into those matters of concern to the White House.

While preparing his examination of Segretti before the grand jury, Federal prosecutor Earl Silbert brought up the matter of "dirty tricks" with Petersen. Petersen related his opinion that Segretti's pranks did not violate the Corrupt Practices Act. Another individual who thought Segretti might have performed criminal acts was the head of the FBI Accounting and Fraud Division, Charley Bowles. Bowles inquired of Petersen if Segretti had violated any election law. Petersen answered that he was not aware of any specific violations by Segretti.

Petersen ordered Silbert not to look into the relationships Segretti had maintained with Chapin, Strachan, and Kalmbach. Petersen said he "didn't want [Silbert] getting into relationships between the President and his lawyer or the fact that the President's lawyer might be involved in somewhat, I thought, illegitimate campaign activities on behalf of the President."

If Petersen was saying that he did not want to tread on the thin ice of lawyer-client privilege relating to Nixon and Kalmbach, he had a point. However, ruling out questioning Segretti about anything having to do with his relationships with Chapin and Strachan was fishy, at best. At worst, it smacked of collusion with the White House.

Segretti flew to Miami Beach a few days prior to his appearance before the grand jury. He met with John Dean on August 20, 1972, the Sunday before the Republican national convention opened. Dean reassured the shaky Segretti that the Federal prosecutors had no interest in probing the Segretti's connections with Chapin, Strachan, and Kalmbach. However, Dean advised Segretti that if anyone asked him about his dirty tricks operation, he should tell the truth. In fact, Dean told Segretti to answer every answer truthfully. Dean told Segretti to give up "the whole ball of wax" if he had to. Of course, at that time, Segretti did not know that Dean wanted to use Nixon's dirty trickster as a sacrificial lamb to protect higher-ups at the White House.

Dean's chief concern was that Kalmbach's name might come up. However, Dean believed he could put "certain parameters on the grand jury examination" through Petersen.

Segretti flew to Washington to testify. Before going before the grand jury, Segretti submitted to an interview conducted by Silbert and Don Campbell of the United States Attorney's Office. At one point, Campbell asked Segretti if a "Mr. K." was paying him. Segretti paused and then answered in the affirmative.

During the questioning before the grand jury, neither Silbert nor Campbell mentioned the name of Segretti's paymaster and he volunteered nothing. Just when it looked as if Segretti would get out of the jury room without having to reveal anything about Chapin, Strachan, and Kalmbach, a female member of the grand jury finally asked him where he got his financing. Segretti followed Dean's advice and told the truth by admitting that Kalmbach had paid him tens of thousands of dollars. Under further probing, Segretti admitted that Chapin and Strachan hired him.

For his part, Earl Silbert denied that the original Watergate prosecutors limited their questioning of Segretti to protect Chapin, Strachan, and Kalmbach, or to conceal the identities of the three men. Silbert argued that since Segretti received his last payment in March 1972, prior to the effective date of the Federal Election Campaign Act of 1971, "it foreclosed the possibility of a violation of this act."

Silbert went into some detail about his questioning of Segretti. He said, "Because none of his non-Watergate activity appeared to involve criminal violations and because the grand jury was investigating only Watergate, we did not examine Mr. Segretti at length about his political spying activities before the grand jury. However, we requested the FBI to interview Messrs. Chapin and Strachan of the White House staff, who Mr. Segretti informed us had recruited him, and Mr. Kalmbach in California. The reports of these interviews were sent to the Special Election Law Unit in the Department of Justice. The possible inference drawn by some that we did not explore Mr. Segretti's spying activities before the grand jury because we wanted to conceal any involvement of Messrs. Kalmbach, Chapman, and Strachan is nonsense."

When a lawyer becomes too legalistic, it is a sure sign that he has no moral ground on which to stand. Silbert's defense of his limited questioning of Segretti was passionate, but it simply does not ring true. The United States Attorney's Office deserved no credit for turning over what the grand jury learned about Chapin, Strachan, and Kalmbach to the FBI. Silbert never intended to ask Segretti about the three men. The information came out only because a grand jury member, not a prosecutor, acted with diligence. In addition, Silbert based his defense of his actions before the grand jury on the fact that Segretti had not committed any discernable crime. Silbert knew better. The truth is that Silbert tried to keep Segretti disconnected from the White House, and he failed.

Following Segretti's testimony before the grand jury, he called John Dean. Segretti told Dean that he had revealed his association with Chapin, Strachan, and Kalmbach. The news bothered Dean. Instead of heading off the investigation as Dean had desired, Segretti's grand jury testimony had expanded it.

Dean realized immediately that the FBI would now want to interview Chapin, Strachan, and Kalmbach. While he had no personal contact with Kalmbach, Dean prepared Chapin and Strachan for their FBI interviews.

Later, Dean said that Strachan volunteered to perjure himself to prevent H. R. Haldeman from becoming involved in the scandal. Strachan contradicted Dean's version of the story. Strachan said he was merely talking about a false report that stated that Haldeman recruited Segretti. Strachan said he would take sole responsibility for hiring the diminutive prankster.

In the middle of September 1972, Carl Bernstein of the *Washington Post* contacted Segretti. Later, Robert Meyers, also of the *Washington Post* got in touch with the dirty trickster. Quivering with fear, Segretti called a college friend of his, Lawrence "Larry" Young for legal advice.

After speaking with Young, Segretti made calls to Dwight Chapin and John Dean. Chapin told Segretti to "get lost" until the heat was off. Dean agreed with Chapin that Segretti should keep out of sight, but he told Segretti to check in with him from time to time.

On October 10, 1972, the *Washington Post* published the first allegations that Segretti had organized a massive campaign of "political spying and sabotage conducted on behalf of

President Nixon's reelection and directed by officials at the White House and the Committee for the Reelection of the President."

Dean called Segretti prior to the publication of the *Washington Post* article. Dean said he was in Florida, but he would fly to Washington as soon as possible and meet with Segretti to discuss the allegations the article raised. Segretti booked a flight to Washington immediately. Upon landing in our nation's capital, he checked into a motel near the airport, and then immediately called Dean's assistant, Fred Fielding.

Fielding ordered Segretti to check out of the motel (Segretti had registered under his real name) and take a taxi to a location about a block away from the Executive Office Building. Fielding was awaiting Segretti when he arrived. Fielding motioned Segretti into a car and then drove him to the Executive Office Building.

Segretti did not sign the logbook while entering the Executive Office Building this time. Fielding told the accommodating guard "this is the individual who lost his wallet." The guard nodded and Fielding and Segretti walked into the building and went into Dean's office. Segretti met with Dean and Fielding for about an hour. During the meeting, the three discussed the allegations contained in the *Washington Post* article.

Dean read the *Washington Post* article to Segretti, allegation by allegation. As Dean read, Segretti commented on the accuracy of each allegation. At the end of the meeting, they talked briefly about Segretti penning a statement for release the following day.

When their meeting ended, Dean ordered Fielding to drive Segretti to a motel near Crystal City, Virginia. There, Segretti checked in under an assumed name.

After a night of fitful sleep, a worried and exhausted Donald Segretti rose early the next morning. Segretti pulled up the well-worn motel chair to the beat up desk in the corner and sat down. He then took a sheet of motel stationary from the desk drawer and scribbled out a short, self-serving statement for possible release by the White House. He should not have bothered.

At about 10 a.m., Fred Fielding arrived at Segretti's motel room. Fielding brought with him a prepared statement for Segretti to review. Fielding said individuals at the White House had worked-up the statement that morning. The statement denied most of the allegations made in the *Washington Post* story. Segretti corrected a few words in the statement and then handed it back to Fielding. Segretti may have made more corrections, had Fielding not hurried him. Fielding said he was under pressure to get the statement out as soon as possible.

Later that day, Dean called Segretti and related that the White House media people had determined that the story would die on its own and that a statement from Segretti was unnecessary at that time. Therefore, the White House would release no comment on the *Washington Post* story.

The decision not to release a statement occurred during the meeting in Dwight Chapin's office in the White House after Fielding returned from Crystal City. Those present at the meeting were Chapin, Ron Ziegler (White House Press Secretary), John Ehrlichman, John Dean, Gordon Strachan, and Fielding.

After the meeting, Ehrlichman directed Dean to order Segretti to go into hiding and to stay away from the press until after the election. Evidently, Ehrlichman didn't know that Segretti was already trying to avoid the prying eyes of America's eagle-eyed media.

Later that afternoon, Dean paid Segretti a visit at the motel in Crystal City. Dean was very cordial and he seemed relaxed, as if it were a social call. During the conversation, Dean hinted that Segretti should leave the country. Dean mentioned, almost offhandedly, how "nice the Greek Islands were that time of year."

Dean and Segretti did not come to an understanding about Segretti leaving the country, but Segretti did heed another suggestion. Dean offered that Segretti should return to California by train. That way, according to Dean's logic, Segretti could avoid nosey reporters who were doubtlessly at the airport swimming around like sharks smelling blood in the water. Segretti took Dean's suggestion as an order. Segretti went to the Washington station, boarded the first available Amtrak passenger train going to Philadelphia, and began his long odyssey across America.

A fretful Segretti road the steel rail in the relative confront the railroad offered from Washington to Philadelphia, from Philadelphia to Chicago, from Chicago to Houston, from Houston to Nevada, and then on to California. He encountered no reporters during his trek.

While winding his way across America, Segretti decided it was a good idea to contact his Florida operatives, Robert Benz and Doug Kelly. Segretti gave the two men his real name for the first time and told them to prepare themselves for the media hurricane headed their way.

While Segretti was keeping out of sight, H. R. Haldeman briefed President Nixon on the situation. Haldeman told Nixon, "Segretti, just so you know, is incommunicado, but he calls John Dean from a public phone and calls on a line that's not traceable every day around noon."

While briefing Nixon, Haldeman expressed a certain admiration for Segretti. He told the President that Segretti would "do anything." Haldeman continued, "I'm told he was supposedly the ideal guy for this kind of thing. He's a guy that loves this sort of college prank politics."

Upon hearing about the *Washington Post* story on Segretti from Haldeman, Nixon wanted to take the offensive. The President suggested that Segretti sue the newspaper. Nixon said, "I know he'll lose it, but good God, in the public mind it creates an impression that they lied . . . Right, Bob? You see the point? Sue the sons of bitches."

During his period of incognito, Segretti kept in regular contact with Dean. Segretti thought Dean was keeping him informed on the latest developments and revelations coming out of the ever-expanding scandal. However, the truth was that Dean was merely keeping tabs on Segretti.

Immediately after the election, Dean asked Haldeman and Ehrlichman to meet with Segretti to determine the extent of involvement Chapin and Strachan had with the prankster. This is interesting in as much as Dean already had full knowledge of Segretti's relationships with Chapin and Strachan. Haldeman and Ehrlichman demurred from meeting with Segretti in person, but they wanted the full details of Segretti's connection to the White House. They ordered Dean to get those details.

A few days after his meeting with Haldeman and Ehrlichman, Dean met with Segretti at the El Dorado Hotel in Palm Springs, California. Segretti had been staying there under an assumed name for about a week. Dean brought a tape recorder to the meeting and took a full confession from Segretti. Dean promised Segretti that "attorney-client privilege" covered the contents of the tape and no court or legal agency had the power to subpoena it for perusal.

Dean was not telling Segretti the truth. Because of Dean's later actions, neither the Senate Watergate Committee nor the Federal courts considered the tape privileged. Had he claimed it, the courts would have found that the facts did not support a bona fide attorney-client relationship between Dean and Segretti. However, Dean never made such a claim to authorities,

Dean could not stay in Palm Springs as long as he wished. On November 11, he received a phone call from White House aide Tod Hullin. Hullin informed him that Haldeman and Ehrlichman, who were in Florida with President Nixon, desired a report on Dean's meeting with Segretti. Further, they wanted Dean to come to Florida and make the report in person.

Understanding the urgency of the situation, Dean caught the next available flight to Florida and met with Haldeman and Ehrlichman on November 12, 1972. At this meeting, Dean played Segretti's taped confession for them. When Dean played the tape for Haldeman and Ehrlichman, he had to know that not only had he violated legal ethics, but also that he had removed any Attorney-client privilege that may have existed between himself and Segretti.

While Dean was briefing Haldeman and Ehrlichman on his Palm Springs meeting with Segretti, Haldeman received a message that Nixon wanted him to come to the President's office. Haldeman sent a message back to the President informing Nixon that he would be over to report on the meeting with Dean and Ehrlichman shortly.

On November 15, 1972, Dean met with Haldeman and Ehrlichman again, this time at the presidential vacation residence at Camp David, Maryland. During the early portion of the meeting, they discussed the subject of firing David Chapin. Haldeman and Ehrlichman told Dean that because of the information contained on the Segretti tape, President Nixon had decided that Chapin had to go.

Other staffers, such as Special Council to the President, Richard Moore, had relayed to Dean that they felt that the President should merely issue a letter of censure to Chapin. When Dean mentioned the possibility of a letter of censure, Haldeman and Ehrlichman shot down the idea. Ehrlichman told Dean that the President wanted the Chapin matter to go away and that Nixon didn't want to hear any more about it. Then, Haldeman and Ehrlichman ordered Dean to fire Chapin immediately. Dean did so soon after the meeting.

The truth is that the President felt some remorse about dumping Dwight Chapin. Chapin had been with Nixon since 1962 and the two saw each other almost every day. Beyond that, Nixon was responsible for Chapin's hiring of Donald Segretti. It was one of the few times that Nixon ever expressed a sense of guilt for anything he did.

Near the end of the meeting, Ehrlichman ordered Dean to get Segretti a job outside the United States. The reason for that order is more than obvious. Ehrlichman did not want Segretti around to do any more testifying.

Dean passed Ehrlichman's directive to get Segretti out of the country on to Herb Kalmbach. Kalmbach moved quickly. He found

Segretti a job at the Holiday Inn in Montego Bay, Jamaica. The job paid a hefty sum of $30,000 (more than $180,000 by today's standards) annually. Segretti's job would have been in public relations and he would have done a little legal work as well.

Segretti turned down Kalmbach's job offer. Segretti had great interest in the high paying position, but, according to him, he "could not" accept it. First, his mother was ill and he did not want to relocate that far away from her. In addition, Segretti had received a subpoena from the Senate Judiciary Subcommittee on Administrative Policies and Procedures and he felt compelled to stay in America and testify. Thus, Segretti declined the comfortable job. Nixon's aides had failed to remove the Segretti thorn from Nixon's side, and the prankster remained a problem for the White House.

Along with everything else, Dean had a conference with Paul O'Brien, Council for the Committee to Reelect the President, about securing a West Coast attorney for Segretti. O'Brien recommended an old friend of his from Los Angeles, Gordon Hampton.

Segretti met with Hampton and at his new lawyer's request, Segretti penned a statement by hand detailing his activities for the past year. Then, on December 8, 1972, Hampton violated Segretti's confidence and legal ethics by sending Segretti's statement, telephone bills, address cards, and bankbook to Paul O'Brien. O'Brien, at Hampton's request passed the materials along to Dean, even though Dean never requested the items directly.

Hampton and O'Brien later contended that they turned the privileged materials over to Dean because they thought he was acting as co-council for Segretti. Dean accepted the documents, and later complied with a subpoena to turn them over to the Senate Committee investigating Watergate chaired by Samuel "Sam" Ervin of North Carolina.

Next, Segretti hired Los Angeles trial attorney John Pollock to help him prepare for his testimony before the Senate Subcommittee on Administrative Practices and Procedures. When Pollock wondered why Segretti had selected him, Gordon Hampton informed Pollock that his name had been "submitted to or screened by or approved by the White House." During the period that Hampton and Pollock represented Segretti, they reported all their activities to John Dean.

Since it is clear that his attorneys were more interested in protecting the White House than in representing Segretti, the prankster certainly didn't get the best defense possible.

19. Segretti Convicted

The investigations into the Watergate affair (by both legal authorities and news outlets) led to Segretti and the slanderous letter accusing Senators Jackson and Humphrey of sexual improprieties led to criminal actions. In May 1973, the United States Attorney's office brought indictments against some of the participants in that particular dirty trick.

In order to get the evidence he needed, the United States Attorney offered Bob Benz immunity and in exchange for his cooperation. He accepted the deal and the prosecutor used his testimony against others, including Segretti. In addition, the Senate committee investigating Watergate heard testimony from Benz and Doug Kelly. They described in detail the fake campaign literature, scurrilous letters, disrupted rallies, and other pranks that came out of Segretti's dirty tricks operation. Their testimony left no doubt that Segretti had committed and suborned criminal acts.

George Hearing, who did nothing beyond mailing the slanderous letter, suffered the worst fate of all Segretti's men. After his indictment on one count of distributing unsigned political literature, Hearing entered a guilty plea and received a one-year prison sentence.

As for Segretti, a grand jury indicted him in Orlando, Florida on May 4, 1973. The charges consisted of two counts of illegal distribution of campaign literature. Segretti entered a plea of not guilty. Then on August 4, 1973, prosecutors superseded the first indictment and replaced it with a new indictment charging Segretti with four counts of conspiracy and three counts of illegal distribution of campaign literature.

With his fellow dirty tricksters willing to testify against him, and the White House doing nothing to help him, Segretti's conviction was certain. However, prosecutors offered Segretti a deal. They promised that if he would enter a guilty plea and testify against Dwight Chapin at Chapin's perjury trial, then they would give him a light sentence. Segretti agreed to the deal. He had no loyalty to his old friend and he had no problem selling Chapin down the river.

On October 1, 1973, Segretti appeared before Federal District Judge Gerhard A. Gesell in Washington and pleaded guilty to three misdemeanor charges (two counts of illegal distribution of campaign literature, and one count of conspiracy). On November 5, the judge sentenced Segretti to six months in prison and three years of probation.

As part of the plea deal, "Watergate Judge" John Sirica signed orders granting Segretti limited immunity from prosecution in exchange for his testimony before the Watergate federal grand jury and the Senate Watergate investigating committee. Segretti did testify against Chapin and he did so with enthusiasm. His testimony aided in greatly Chapin's conviction.

Leon Jaworski, the Special Prosecutor with the Watergate Special Prosecution Force, wrote, ". . . Very early in our office's investigation of this matter . . . Segretti agreed to supply us with any information and cooperate fully with our efforts. Since that time we have interviewed him on various occasions, he has testified in the grand jury and was a government witness in the perjury prosecution of . . . Chapin. In all his appearances we believe that . . . Segretti has been totally truthful and candid both as to the relevant facts and his feelings of remorse for his involvement."

In other words, Segretti was a prize rat.

On November 12, 1973, Segretti surrendered to authorities at Lompoc Prison Camp in California. The minimum-security prison had the nickname "Camp Cupcake." The camp, about 150 miles north of Los Angeles was a prison in the broadest sense of the word only. The 350 or so inmates served their time in a facility with no fences or locks, the inmates were on the "honor system," and they were free to walk around the grounds unsupervised. Segretti received parole after serving four and a half months at Camp Cupcake.

More important to Segretti than a short term in a comfortable prison was his future. Segretti knew the state of California had the power to disbar him for life and the prospect of losing his career horrified him. When he received a letter from the California Bar Association saying it is considering disbarring him, he said, "Four months in Lompoc is nothing to me compared to being disbarred. What would I do?"

The court referred the Segretti matter to the California State Bar "for a hearing and report as to whether the facts and circumstances surrounding the offenses involved moral turpitude or other misconduct warranting discipline and, if so found, for a recommendation as to discipline."

The board assembled by the California State Bar found that Segretti's acts "involved moral turpitude or other misconduct warranting discipline." The board members could not agree on the extent of the discipline, however.

One thing that kept the board from voting unanimously to disbar Segretti for life was his admission of guilt. Segretti testified before the Senate Watergate Committee "my activities were wrong and have no place in the American political system. To the extent the activities have harmed other persons and the political process, I have the deepest regret." In addition, his cooperation with the Special Prosecutor's Office in helping to take down Chapin benefited Segretti before the California Bar Association.

The California Bar Association did not disbar Segretti for life. Instead, on February 27, 1976, it merely suspended his license for two years. Once reinstated, he resumed his legal practice in California and he has remained in good standing with the California Bar Association since.

20. Financing Segretti

Segretti took his job seriously and he threw himself into his work with great enthusiasm. The overanxious young man kept a frenetic pace and followed an exhausting schedule. In his first 6 months on the job, he visited at least 16 states and contacted more than 80 individuals in his effort to build up his nationwide dirty tricks organization.

Of course, Segretti concentrated on states he and his managers thought were important. Although he went elsewhere, he put most of his efforts and money into about a dozen or so key states.

Segretti spent thousands of "untraceable" dollars he received from Herbert Kalmbach while crisscrossing America, but he spent less than he received. Between the time when he took the first two checks from Kalmbach on September 29, 1971 and when he received his last payment on March 23, 1972 (9 days after the Florida presidential primary), Kalmbach paid him a total of $45,336. In that same period of almost 6 months, Segretti claimed he spent $22,424. Almost $9,000 of that went to 30 or so individuals that Segretti referred to as his "operatives."

It is interesting that Segretti never explained where the other almost $23,000 (more than half he received) went. Theodore H. White opined, without proof, that Segretti "pocketed" the additional thousands, but this author doubts that he kept very much for himself beyond his salary.

More likely, Segretti was just sloppy with his bookkeeping and he didn't always keep track of what he spent. For instance, he certainly did not list everyone he paid for helping him his pranks. In addition, his accounting stops in March 1972, but Segretti continued his operation for another three months. Thus, there were certainly expenditures for which Segretti neglected to account.

Segretti's list of the monies he received and spent in the course of his dirty tricks work for Nixon follows below:

RECEIPTS

September 29, 1971: $667

September 29, 1971: $5,000

October 19, 1971: $667

October 27, 1971: $667

November 11, 1971: $667

November 29, 1971: $667

December 13, 1971: $667

December 27, 1971: $667

January 15, 1972: $5,000

January 17, 1972: $667

March 1, 1972: $5,000

March 23, 1972: $25,000

TOTAL: $45,336

EXPENSES

Travel: $6,029.52

Telephone: $2,099.56

Printing and Mailing: $1,816.43

Accommodations: $1,555.80

Meals: $616.88

Office expenses: $1,331.39

SUBTOTAL: $13,439.37

Payments to Operatives: $8,984.70

TOTAL: $22,424.07

UNACCOUNTED FOR: $22,911.93

21. Segretti's Operatives

Segretti enlisted a large number of persons to help him in his dirty tricks operation. He admitted to asking more than 80 individuals to aid in his dirty tricks operation. Beyond that, some of Segretti's agents hired others. Considering this, it is possible that the number recruited to aid in Segritti's dirty tricks scheme surpassed 100.

Along with paying his "pranksters" – as he sometimes called them – Segretti promised some of those who joined his operation "big jobs" in Washington after President Nixon's reelection. It is doubtful that Segretti could have delivered on any of those big jobs he offered, but those whom he hired evidently did not know that.

We will never have a complete list because Segretti never revealed all the names. He said that he could not remember the names of some of the eighty odd persons he contacted and he refused to surrender the names of those he considered "completely innocent." In fact, Segretti only mentioned those who helped him when he had to do so. However, evidence exists proving that more than thirty persons received payments from Segretti. However, the reader should understand that perhaps scores of others took part in the operation, but remain unknown. In addition, full names of some of the conspirators are unknown.

Joe Arriola: Produced printed materials for some of Segretti's dirty tricks, E. Howard Hunt ordered Segretti to make use of Arriola.

He received an unknown amount in payment from Segretti, but it likely came close to $2,000.

Bob Benz: Benz was the President of the Tampa Young Republicans Club. Benz aided the dirty tricks operation in several states. Segretti paid Benz at least $2,417 for his part in the scheme.

Jess Burdick: Segretti paid Burdick $335 for keeping Senator under surveillance.

[?] Collins: Segretti paid Collins at least $5.

Duke (actual name unknown): Duke, a Nazi, aided the dirty tricks operation in Florida. He received an unknown amount in payment from Segretti.

Kip Edwards: Edwards aided the dirty tricks operation in Florida. He received an unknown amount in payment from Segretti.

[?] Frias: Segretti paid Frias at least $20.

Eselene Frolich: Frolich infiltrated the Jackson campaign in Florida. She received an unknown amount in payment from Segretti.

Bobby Garner: Garner aided in the dirty tricks operation in Texas. Segretti paid him at least $265.

[?] Grantz: Segretti paid Grantz at least $50.

Peg Griffin: Griffin infiltrated the Muskie campaign in Florida. She received a salary of $75 per week (hundreds of dollars total) from the Segretti operation.

[?] Hayes: Segretti paid Hayes at least $31.50.

George Hearing: Hearing aided the dirty tricks operation in Florida. He received an unknown amount in payment from Segretti.

Doug Kelly: Kelly was a member of the Young Republican Club in Florida. He aided the dirty tricks operation in several states. Segretti paid him at least $3,436.

Michael Martin: Martin aided the dirty tricks operation in New York. Segretti paid him at least $122.

[?] Miller: Segretti paid Miller at least $22.

Bob Nieley: Nieley aided the dirty tricks in Pennsylvania. Segretti paid him at least $10.

James Norton: Norton aided the dirty tricks operation in California. Segretti paid him at least $451.20

Pat O'Brien: O'Brien infiltrated the Muskie campaign in California. Segretti paid him at least $40.

[?] Oldham: Segretti paid Oldham at least $20.

Jim Popovich: Segretti hired Popovich to aid in the dirty tricks operation in California. Segretti paid him at least $130.

Al Reece: Reece aided the dirty tricks operation in Florida. He received an unknown amount in payment from Segretti.

[?] Sarhad: Segretti paid Sarhad at least $165.

Mike Silva: Silva aided the Dirty tricks operation in California. Segretti paid him at least $140.

[?] Staub: Segretti paid Staub at least $50.

Charles Svihlik: Svihlik aided the dirty tricks operation in several states. Segretti paid him at least $200.

University of Florida student (name unknown): She aided the dirty tricks operation in Florida. Segretti paid her at least $20.

Ward Turnquist: Turnquist worked for Segretti in Southern California. Segretti paid him at least $80.

Tom Visney: Visney aided the dirty tricks operation in several states. Segretti paid him at least $710.

"Mr. Yancy" (actual name unknown): Yancy aided the dirty tricks operation in Florida. He received an unknown amount in payment from Segretti.

Skip Zimmer: Zimmer aided the dirty tricks operation in Pennsylvania. Segretti paid him at least $255.

22. A Rinky-Dink Operation?

Several individuals disparaged Segretti's covert operation before and after it became public. Below are a few of the things persons said or wrote:

Theodore H. White opined that Segretti's dirty tricks operation "had the weight of a feather in the internal struggle of the Democratic Party."

Republican Senator Edward J. Gurney of Florida, a member of the Senate Watergate Committee called Segretti's activities "a rinky-dink operation."

E. Howard Hunt characterized Segretti's dirty tricks as "sophomoric."

G. Gordon Liddy and others referred Segretti's pranks as "rat fucking."

One Federal investigator said Segretti was "just a small fish in a big pond."

Even President Nixon got into the act. He said the Segretti was merely playing "chicken shit games."

As for Segretti, he once said it was "nickel and dime stuff."

One could accept the statements above had Segretti simply engaged in harmless, isolated, and minor pranks. However, he willingly crossed the line of decency, engaged in character assassinations, and committed other crimes. His antics led to hard feelings among some of the Democrats and they did affect the nominating process.

The hard feelings some of the other Democratic candidates developed for George McGovern caused them to do little or nothing for him in the fall campaign. As we have seen, much of the hard feelings generated came, not from McGovern, but from Segretti.

George McGovern's 1972 National Campaign Director, Frank Mankiewicz, put it this way, "We [the McGovern and Humphrey campaigns] were no longer opponents; we had become enemies. And I think largely as a result of this [Segretti's] activity."

23. Did Segretti Succeed?

The question as to whether the Segretti enterprise was successful is still a matter of some debate. It should not be. The black advance operation and other actions of the Segretti group succeeded in its primary mission.

In his book *The Making of the President 1972*, venerable political author, and historian, Theodore H. White opined that Segretti and his pranksters did not affect the Democratic Party's nominating process. He said the dirty tricks operation "had the weight of a feather in the internal struggle of the Democratic Party."

White was a brilliant man, but he was wrong in this instance – at least to some degree. While other factors were certainly involved, Segretti's covert dirty tricks effort achieved all its goals:

(1) Damage or destroy the Muskie campaign.

(2) Cause such discord in the Democratic Party that the eventual nominee could not unite it.

(3) Engineer the nomination of Nixon's weakest rival, George McGovern.

The success of Segretti's operation at infiltrating various Democratic campaigns contributed to disrupting and harassing those candidates.

One of Segretti's most successful efforts in disrupting the campaigns of the Democratic candidates was the dissemination of false or misleading literature. The transmittal of fake literature took place in nearly every state that held a meaningful primary in 1972.

The words of Senator George McGovern's 1972 National Campaign Director, Frank Mankiewicz, are worth repeating, "We [the McGovern and Humphrey campaigns] were no longer opponents; we had become enemies. And I think largely as a result of this [Segretti's] activity."

In addition, Senator Muskie and his staff blamed Senators McGovern, Humphrey, and their supporters for much of the scurrilous literature Segretti disturbed in the primary states.

The false literature helped fracture an already fragile Democratic Party. McGovern, not Nixon, shouldered the blame for many of the dirty tricks performed by Segretti and others working on behalf of the President. This being the case, it was impossible for McGovern to patch the fissure in the party after he won the nomination from the establishment Democrats.

Segretti's false and misleading radio and newspaper ads created confusion among voters and the various Democratic campaigns. The small anti-Muskie advertisements placed by Segretti and his lackeys in selected states proved successful as well. They did not cost Muskie more than a smattering of votes in any state, but they did cause ill will among the Democratic presidential candidates. Muskie believed the ads were the work of his opponents and some of his staffers said so publicly. When the accused candidates heard this, they reacted with indignation.

The undeniable fact is that Segretti succeeded splendidly with the forged Barbara Barron letters and the fake letters placing the blame for them on Mayor Yorty. The letters caused anger, undermined any trust the Democratic candidates may have had for each other, and widened the gulf between the various Democratic candidates.

24. Segretti's Slithering

Donald Segretti, as do most persons caught in wrongful acts, attempted to deny some of them, and to defend others. He continues to deny and defend certain of his acts to this day.

This chapter explores some of Segretti's statements in which he defended his actions, or painted himself as a victim. These statements come from various reliable sources including email exchanges between Mr. Segretti and the author.

Segretti: Segretti feels that he has "been abused by rumor, character assassination, innuendo, and a complete disregard for the privacy of myself, my friends, and my family." He also claims that members of the media illegally obtained his phone, bank and credit card records.

The Truth: Segretti was correct in that he was the victim of abuse, rumor, character assassination, innuendo, and a complete disregard for his privacy. In short, others did to him exactly what he did to his victims. Because of his disregard of others, Segretti's claims that he is a victim ring hollow.

Segretti: Segretti proclaimed the following loudly: "I would like to state . . . that at no time did I ever have any knowledge of, nor did I participate in, the Watergate burglary or any activity involving electronic surveillance."

The Truth: Segretti did not take part in the Watergate break-in. Neither did he, as far as has been established by fact, partake in any activity involving "electronic surveillance." He *did* take part in surveillance, however. The fact that he employed one type of surveillance and not another does not make him any less guilty.

Segretti: Segretti felt that John Dean had assumed the duties as his attorney, but in light of what happened, Segretti said, "I feel that Mr. Dean betrayed my confidence."

The Truth: In this instance, Segretti was correct. Not only did Dean betray Segretti's confidence, Dean attempted to get the White House to use Segretti as a scapegoat. However, the criminality of the White House was so broad and deep that throwing Segretti under the bus did not deflect the investigation. That being said, Dean's actions did not relieve Segretti of the responsibility for *his* actions.

Segretti: When asked why he did what he did, Segretti answered under oath: "I think there were a combination of factors . . . I think it was the individuals who contacted me; the fact that they were old friends; the fact that I had – still have – respect for them, even though a lot of water has gone under the bridge. I think the fact of, in a sense, working for high officials, that is, the White House – I think that was a factor. I think the fact that it was at a particular stage in my life; the Army was not a career that I wanted to pursue. I was in it for the period of time that I was obligated, to do the best job I could in the military, but after that I wanted to go out and do something else. There was a change of pace from that and it sounded like a great deal of travel, and I think those are all factors that must be listed."

The Truth: Segretti could have shortened his statement considerably by just telling the exact truth – he was willing to commit crimes for his own personal gain. Additionally, his testimony against Chapin in exchange for a lighter sentence did not indicate that he had any respect for his old friend. Like so many of those that committed crimes for Nixon, once caught, Segretti was more than willing to give up the "whole ball of wax" in selling out his friends.

Segretti: Segretti said under oath that G. Gordon Liddy and E. Howard Hunt had "extremely limited knowledge" of his activities.

The Truth: The admission itself is telling. It proves that Segretti was under the umbrella of the "intelligence gathering" operation of Liddy and Hunt. What Liddy knew is unclear, but Hunt had a great deal of knowledge about Segretti's dirty tricks. Indeed, Hunt devised some of them.

Segretti related one instance when Hunt made a request of him regarding a Muskie fundraiser in Washington on April 17, 1972. Segretti said, "Mr. Hunt called me on the telephone and told me about a Muskie dinner in Washington, D.C. and asked me if I would be willing to comeback to Washington, D.C. and do some activities in relation to that dinner." Segretti obliged Hunt.

Segretti: Segretti said he followed no overall game plan in connection with his dirty tricks operation. He stated that he came up with the tricks "over a few beers." He continued that he planned none of his dirty tricks beforehand.

The Truth: The spelling in some of the materials Segretti produced was so horrendous that one could imagine that a drunkard could have devised them. That notwithstanding, Dwight Chapin *did* give Segretti a general game plan to follow, and the trickster followed it as best he could. Segretti's first objective was to damage Edmund Muskie, Chapin ordered him to tailor his dirty tricks to accomplish that goal.

As to the planning of his dirty tricks, Segretti admitted under oath that he provided Dwight Chapin some of the details of his dirty tricks "a day or two" in advance. This is proof that he did plan his dirty tricks beforehand.

Segretti: When this author asked Segretti about his dirty tricks operation, he responded, "I never viewed it as sinister. That is the rhetoric of the progressive left."

The Truth: Some of Segretti's actions were not sinister, others were. For instance, his false accusations against Senators Humphrey and Jackson, and Representative Chisholm were disgusting and certainly sinister. In addition, his forging documents qualify as sinister. While we may be able to rightly criticize America's "progressive left" for many things, their "rhetoric" did not cause Segretti to engage in character assassinations or his other crimes.

Segretti made the choice to break the law on his own, and independently of anyone else.

Segretti: When this author asked Segretti about his crimes, he grew agitated. Segretti responded, "Look at what I violated – I did not realize it was a crime."

The Truth: Segretti was an attorney, and by all accounts, a good one. His statement that he did not "realize" that his activities were criminal was disingenuous. He knew that many of his acts were crimes. Besides that, as the old saying goes, "Ignorance of the law is no excuse."

Segretti: When asked if he thought his punishment for his crimes was too severe, Segretti responded, "I will leave it to others to judge – but I served my country well in Vietnam – was awarded the bronze star, army commendation medal, and air medal. I was drafted into the Army. Never, never was I anything but an American that was from a middle-class family that worked hard that wanted the best for my country. The violations were misdemeanors."

The Truth: Segretti pleaded guilty to three misdemeanor counts and he served a little over four months in a minimum-security prison ("Camp Cupcake"). However, some of the acts for which he had responsibility, were felonies. For instance, forging signatures are felonies and his operation forged signatures. The fact that he was not charged with felonies does not mean he didn't commit them.

As to Segretti's military record, most of those with good military records never engage in criminal acts. His military service did not give Segretti a license to break the law.

Segretti: Segretti still denies he had anything to do with the infamous "Canuck Letter." Segretti also denies any knowledge of the identity of the person that sent the letter to the Manchester *Union Leader*.

The Truth: The circumstantial evidence indicates that someone associated with Segretti most likely sent the letter. The Canuck Letter bore a Florida postmark and that it dovetailed neatly with what Segretti and his flunkies were trying to accomplish. Yet, as difficult as it is to believe, Segretti claims he never asked any of his lackeys if one of them sent it. This author finds it impossible to believe that Segretti had no interest in who sent the Canuck Letter.

Segretti did admit to this author that an associate of his could have created and mailed the letter to New Hampshire.

Segretti: In 1973, Segretti expressed remorse for his acts. In fact, he remarked on the subject several times. He said, "Looking back on it, it is not a – none of these activities, I believe, are ones that should be included in the American political system."

Another time Segretti admitted he released deceptive statements to the press and ascribed them to various Democratic candidates. He said about those statements, "I think it is improper and I don't think incorrect distortions, untruths or anything of that nature should be disseminated by the press or by any individual."

Segretti's thoughts on the subject grew even stronger. He continued, "I believe that both parties and all candidates should run in the future – that may run in the future – should look at themselves in a very critical light and any activity such as what I was engaged in, or others may have been engaged in, should not take place."

On still another occasion, Segretti expressed regret for his days as a dirty tricks artist. He said, "There is many a morning that I have waked up and I have said to myself 'I wish I had stayed away,' or I wish I had . . . [someone] sit down with me and say, 'Don, do you really want to get involved in things like this? . . .'"

The Truth: The above sentiments sound contrite, almost noble. Indeed, they may reflect how Segretti felt in 1973, but he does not feel that way now. During this author's conversations with Segretti, the dirty trickster did not express any remorse at all. In fact, it seems that he does not see anything wrong with what he did. He is more interested in blaming others for sullying his reputation than he is for accepting the least responsibility for his actions.

Segretti: Segretti still claims that he was not aware that other dirty tricksters were also running covert for the Nixon campaign.

The Truth: It is possible that Segretti was so dense that he did not know another operation existed. However, one wonders why he never suspected G. Gordon Liddy and E. Howard Hunt of running separate "black ops" for the benefit of Nixon's reelection. After all, Hunt did give Segretti instructions regarding certain dirty tricks.

Segretti: Segretti said that when he accepted $16,000 a year plus expenses for the opportunity "to have fun and travel around for a year" helping Nixon's reelection campaign, his job was not spelled out to him.

The Truth: Very early on Chapin detailed Segretti's mission and Segretti understood that was to be a Republican version of Dick Tuck.

Segretti: Segretti continues to maintain that "99 percent of the stuff" he did during his dirty tricks operation was "perfectly legal."

The Truth: Segretti committed scores of acts that were immoral, unethical, and illegal, His disingenuous attempts to minimize them reflects on his character – or rather, his lack thereof.

Segretti: Speaking of his operation Segretti said, "I thought it was normal. I thought this was done in politics. I guess I was naive. I guess I was not that conversant with political campaigns."

The Truth: Segretti knew exactly what he was doing. He was conversant with the law and he knew right from wrong. It is impossible to believe that Segretti didn't know that character assassination, stealing campaign documents, disrupting events, and unauthorized entries were against the law.

25. Conspiracy Theories

While Donald Segretti did many despicable things, he did not do some things of which others accused him. In fact, to this day, conspiracy theories about Segretti continue to pop up from time to time like new stinkweeds in a garden already full of stinkweeds. Below is a very brief sampling of some of those false accusations made against Segretti. They do not deserve any more exposure than a short recounting.

Segretti and Nixon

There is a rather recent story that Segretti and President Nixon were acquainted before Segretti unleashed his dirty tricks program on the Democrats. They were not. The two never met at any time before or after Chapin hired Segretti.

The evidence is that Nixon did not have a clue as to the identity of Segretti until after the Watergate break-in. The evidence also indicates that when H. R. Haldeman informed the President about Segretti and told Nixon about a number of Segretti's dirty tricks, Nixon lambasted Segretti's operation and called it "chicken shit."

Apparently, the conspiracy theory grew out of the fact that Segretti worked for the Office of the Comptroller of Currency briefly before he went into the Army. However, he was so far down the food chain when he worked in

Washington that Nixon would not have had any reason to meet with him.

Segretti the Bagman

There is another story that Segretti delivered hundreds of thousands of dollars to Nixon's attorney, Herbert Kalmbach from wealthy individuals as payment for ambassadorships and other high offices within the Nixon Administration. The false accusation is that Segretti delivered $60,000 to Kalmbach from each of those attempting to purchase an ambassadorship.

There is no evidence that Segretti ever picked up any large sum of money from anyone, for any reason, and then delivered it to Kalmbach.

Segretti told this author that the idea that he was a bagman and that he delivered bribes to Kalmbach was "nonsense." Based on the evidence, in this instance, Segretti was telling the truth in this instance.

The Karl Rove Connection

Karl Rove was President George W. Bush's primary political consultant and he is still something of a Bogeyman to a large contingent of American Progressives. Some of Rove's opponents have accused him of things so ridiculous that few persons listen to them any longer.

Sometime after Rove ended his relationship with President Bush in 2007, a story flamed up that Rove had led a large, criminal enterprise in

1972 on the behalf of President Nixon's reelection campaign, that Segretti was a part of that endeavor, and that he answered directly to Rove.

The story is wholly false. In 1972, Rove was President-elect of the College Republicans and far from directing Segretti, Rove complained about Segretti's activities in Wisconsin and attempted unsuccessfully to get Segretti fired.

The evidence is clear that Segretti never worked for Rove and never took orders from the future political advisor either.

Segretti confirmed to this author that he never worked for Rove.

The Segretti Spy School

Lawrence Young was another friend and classmate of Segretti's at the University of Southern California. Young was also somewhat acquainted with Dwight Chapin and Gordon Strachan. Young surprised Segretti, who thought they were close friends, when he told reporters from the *Washington Post* that Segretti ran a "spy school" somewhere in the Midwestern United States. The allegation had no truth to it.

Later, Young wrote Segretti a letter of apology and said he only did what he did because *Washington Post* reporters were blackmailing him. Evidently, Segretti did not believe Young. It is good that he did not because Young's assertion that reporters blackmailed him had any truth to them either.

Hunt and Segretti in New York

There are two confirmed meetings and several confirmed telephone conversations between Segretti and E. Howard Hunt. However, there were persistent rumors that the two got together in New York City between their two actual meetings. Both Hunt and Segretti denied that a New York meeting occurred. There is no evidence that the two dirty tricksters ever met in New York.

26. Segretti's Later Life

After getting out of jail and serving his suspension, Segretti returned to the practice of law. He has led a mostly quiet existence out of the spotlight since.

However, each time Segretti has stepped out of his cocoon obscurity, his previous career as a dirty trickster has haunted him. More than two decades after his work as an agent provocateur for Nixon, Segretti decided to seek election to the bench. In 1995, he announced that he would run for Superior Court Judge in Orange County, California.

Immediately upon his announcement, there was a firestorm of opposition to Segretti. Voters do not forget easily and when Segretti announced his intention of seeking a position on the bench, they let their lingering anger over Segretti's past come through vociferously.

Within a week of throwing his hat into the ring, Segretti bowed out of the contest. He conceded that the bitter memories of Watergate smothered his campaign before it got hardly began. Segretti said, "It was supposed to be a low-key campaign and a non-partisan office, but it wasn't treated that way."

The aborted campaign for the judgeship did not completely chill Segretti to politics. In 2000, he served as co-chair of Senator John McCain's presidential campaign in Orange County, California. Working for McCain caused less controversy than his quest for elective office had, but it did cause some. Being associated with Segretti may have cost McCain a small number of votes. Regardless, George W. Bush defeated McCain in the California primary and went on to serve two terms as President. Segretti has not taken any public role in politics since 2000.

Conclusion

When the American people learned of Segretti's dirty tricks operation, a prosecutor called Segretti and his agents "despicable" and "indescribable." The prosecutor said, "You're dealing with people who act like this is Dodge City, not the capital of the United States." It is difficult to disagree with him.

There are those that contend that what Nixon and his cronies did was mild by today's standards. This author agrees that there is a lot of rough stuff going on now. But does posting 100 angry tweets a day measures up to the character assassination practiced by Donald Segretti? This author doesn't think so.

The crimes of Nixon and his agents shook the United States to its very core. Before Watergate, most Americans believed that although the language during campaigns might become angry and hardball politics might be rough, politicians played mostly by the rules. Americans believed that candidates, especially those already in office, respected the system under which they hoped to win election. Watergates proved that was not always the case,

Watergate was just the tip of an iceberg of corruption and deceit that caused many, perhaps most, citizens to lose faith in the American system of self-government. All this time later, the American people still have a general mistrust of their government, regardless of the person, the party, or the ideology in power. That mistrust hampers efficient government. That is Richard Nixon's – and Donald Segretti's – lasting legacy.

Selected Sources

Books

Aitken, Jonathan. *Nixon: A Life*. New York: Regnery History, 1993.

Ambrose, Stephen E. *Nixon: The Triumph of a Politician 1962-1972*. New York: Simon and Shuster, 1989.

Berstein, Carl and Bob Woodward. *All the President's Men*. New York: Simon and Shuster, 1974

Colodny, Len, and Gettlin, Robert. *Silent Coup: The Removal of a President*. New York: St. Martin's Press, 1991.

Drew, Elizabeth. *Washington Journal: Reporting Watergate and Richard Nixon's Downfall*. New York: Overlook Duckworth, 2014.

Gammon, CL. *McGovern-Eagleton '72: A Crazy Train Wreck*. CreateSpace Independent Publishing Platform, 2016.

Gammon, CL. *Seven Candidates for President in 1972*. CreateSpace Independent Publishing Platform, 2014.

Germond, Jack, and Jules Witcover. *Whose Broad Stripes and Bright Stars?, The Trivial Pursuit of the Presidency, 1988*. New York: Warner Books, 1989.

Haldeman, H. R. *The Haldeman Diaries: Inside the White House*. New York: G. P. Putnam Sons, 1994.

Jaworski, Leon. *The Right and the Power.* New York: Reader's Digest Press, 1976

Liddy, G. Gordon. *Will: The Autobiography of G. Gordon Liddy.* New York: St. Martin's Press, 1980.

Nixon, Richard M.: *RN: The Memoirs of Richard Nixon.* New York: Grosset and Dunlap, 1978.

Perlstein, Rick. *Nixonland.* New York: Scribner, 2008.

Reeves, Richard. *President Nixon: Alone in the White House.* New York: Simon and Shuster, 2001

Rosenbaum, David E. "Segretti Describes Chapin As Boss of 'Dirty Tricks'." *New York Times,* October 4, 1973.

Rove, Karl. *Courage and Consequence: My Life as a Conservative in the Fight.* New York: Threshold Editions (a Division of Simon and Shuster), 2010

Small, Melvin. *The Presidency of Richard Nixon.* Lawrence, Kansas: The University of Kansas Press, 1999

Summers, Anthony. *The Arrogance of Power: The Secret World of Richard Nixon.* New York: Penguin Books, 2000.

Thomas, Evan. *Being Nixon: A Man Divided.* New York: Random House, 2015.

Weil, Gordon L. *The Long Shot: George McGovern Runs for President.* New York: W. W. Norton & Company, 1973.

Weiner, Tim. *One Man Against the World.* New York: Henry Holt and Company, 2015.

White, Theodore H. *The Making of the President 1960.* New York: Harper Perennial; Reissue edition, 2010.

White, Theodore H. *The Making of the President 1964.* New York: Harper Perennial; Reissue edition, 2010.

White, Theodore H. *The Making of the President 1968.* New York: Harper Perennial; Reissue edition, 2010.

White, Theodore H. *The Making of the President 1972.* New York: Harper Perennial; Reissue edition, 2010

Wicker, Tom. *One of Us: Richard Nixon and the American Dream.* New York: Random House, 1991.

Witcover, Jules. *Marathon: The Pursuit of the Presidency 1972-1976.* New York: Viking, 1977.

Periodicals

Berstein, Carl and Bob Woodward. "FBI Finds Nixon Aides Sabotaged Democrats." *Washington Post*, Tuesday, October 10, 1972

Berstein, Carl and Bob Woodward. "News Analysis: Still Secret – Who Hired Spies and Why?" *Washington Post*, January 31, 1973.

Crewdson, John M. "Out of Prison a Month, Segretti Tries to Pick Up the Pieces of His Old Carefree Life." *New York Times*, April 22, 1974

Crewdson, John M. "Sabotaging the G.O.P.'s Rivals: Story of a $100,000 Operation." *New York Times*, July 9, 1973.

"From Dirty Trickster to Your Honor?: Mind-boggling: Watergate's Donald H. Segretti is proposed for Orange County judgeship." *Los Angeles Times*. December 11, 1995

Meyer, Lawrence, and Peter A. Jay. "Segretti Bares Dirty Ticks." *Washington Post*, October 4, 1973.

Pincus, Walter. "Drippings from the Watergate." *The New Republic*, July 27, 1973.

Rawlings, Nate. "Donald Segretti and the Nixon Gang." *Time*, January 18, 2012.

Rosenbaum, David E. "Segretti Describes Chapin as Boss of Dirty Tricks." *New York Times*, October 4, 1973.

"Segretti Starts 6-Month Sentence at Federal Prison on Coast." *New York Times*, November 13, 1973.

Witcover, Jules. "'Canuck Episode': A '72 Dirty Trick." *Washington Post*, September 23, 1973.

Other Sources

Final Report of the Select Committee on Presidential Campaign Activities United States Senate, The. Washington: U.S. Government Printing Office, June 1974.

Gammon, CL. An unpublished series of email conversations with Donald Segretti, August-September, 2019.

Gammon, CL. An unpublished series of email conversations with Gordon E. Weil, August-September 2019.

About the Author

CL Gammon has had a life-long fascination with American History and with the written word. These joint fascinations have led to his becoming an award winning and an internationally known bestselling author of more than fifty books. Gammon, who studied Political Science at Tennessee Technological University and History and Government at Hillsdale College, has entertained and educated readers for more than a decade. Several universities, including the State University of New York and the University of Akron, have employed his books as course material. In addition, articles written by Gammon have appeared in more than a dozen national and regional publications. He also writes features for his hometown newspaper, the *Macon County Times*. Gammon lives in Lafayette, Tennessee with his family.

Name Index

www.ingramcontent.com/pod-product-compliance
Lightning Source LLC
Chambersburg PA
CBHW071511150726
48000CB00002B/530